BLUE COLLAR *Faith*

B.A. BRIGHTLIGHT

BE A BRIGHT LIGHT
FOR THE LORD!
MATT 5:16

ISBN: 1453667555
ISBN-13: 9781453667552

Table of Contents

Introduction

Welcome to Blue Collar Faith. This is a collection of stories from ordinary people sharing the extraordinary experience of living a life in service to our Lord Jesus Christ. As the title implies, the contributing authors are not preachers, Bible scholars, or theologians, but are "blue collar" in their walk of faith; they pick up their lunch pail and head to their job, vocation, or "other duties as assigned." They are businessmen and women, retirees, military generals, and stay-at-home moms.

There is no set format to what they have written. It may be a personal story, an observation, a simple spiritual point, or a deep theological pondering devoted to applying the wisdom of the Scriptures to everyday life. The authors' objective is to share their perspective on being salt and light in the world, serving and encouraging one another individually, as a nation, and as the body of Christ and promoting the Good News of the Gospel.

The book is dedicated to the glory of God. The majority of the proceeds from its sale will be donated to participating churches and organizations to provide supplies to those in unfortunate and even desperate situations. It is intended to give the reader food for thought, and the funds it generates will provide food, supplies, and mission support to those in need, both in the local community and abroad.

So get comfortable and enjoy the book, and we hope that God will use it to fill your heart with encouragement, insight, and peace.

1. Six Minutes to Midnight

In a remote desert area of New Mexico during the pre-dawn hours of July 16, 1945, a group of American scientists and observers witnessed a world-changing event. The first test of an atomic weapon lit up the horizon in a flash of brilliant light. Humanity had unleashed the power of the atom, and the Atomic Age was born.

The energy capacity discovered in this tiny building block of matter was enormous, and this power had incredible potential for good–as well as absolute evil. Three weeks later, the Allies used this destructive force on fellow human beings in the bombing of the Japanese cities of Hiroshima and Nagasaki with gruesome effects. It quickly ended the war in the Pacific, but at a cost of over 200,000 lives—people who died either directly from the blasts or from excessive exposure to radiation. Although the creation of this weapon probably saved millions of lives by ending the conflict and making the invasion of Japan unnecessary, America had gained the distinction of introducing the planet to the ghastly power of the atomic bomb.

The world has never been the same. Humankind now possessed the capacity to destroy itself in an instant.

This paradigm-shifting technology created the Cold War, with two primary superpowers engaged in a global-power chess game restrained only by the threat of mutual annihilation. This standoff had a very appropriate acronym: MAD—Mutually Assured Destruction. The Soviet Union and America had so many nuclear weapons that they could assure total destruction of the world many times over. To represent this imminent threat, a picture of a clock called the "Doomsday Clock" was created by the board of directors of the *Bulletin of Atomic Scientists* in 1947 to track the world's proximity to global disaster. Midnight was defined as the moment of catastrophe. Over its history, the clock has advanced or regressed dependent upon the world's political environment. It started at seven minutes to midnight and has ranged from two minutes to midnight in 1953 (when both the Soviet Union and the United States initiated thermonuclear tests) to seventeen minutes to midnight in 1991 when the Strategic Arms Reduction Treaty was signed between the United States and Russia, signaling the end of the Cold War.[1]

Currently, the clock sits at six minutes to midnight—not much time for us Cinderellas. Initially, the Doomsday Clock was intended to monitor the threat of global nuclear war, but it now includes the threats of terrorism, biological or germ warfare, flu or virus pandemics, and global warming.

This is the way the world is. Despite all of the advances of the human race over the last seventy years—the gains in science, medicine, food production, the advent of powerful computers, and the many other improvements the world has made, we all sit precipitously close to annihilation. Though a global war between large armies seems slightly more remote, terrorism has virtually assured us that low-intensity conflicts will remain with us for a very long time, if not until the *end* of time. What's most unnerving is that widespread death and destruction is not confined to the battlefield. Like a blood cancer within our global society, it can happen or manifest itself almost anywhere at any time.

Also very concerning are the manically led regimes such as Iran, which is in an all-out pursuit of a nuclear weapon, or North Korea, which already has one. They definitely threaten their regions with chaos that could easily blossom into a global crisis.

If this isn't enough to plunge one into planetary gloom, misery, and angst, consider that the world is suffering from an economic crisis as well. Many nations have dangerous levels of debt. If merely a few begin to default on their loans, it could cause a domino effect that would create a global financial crisis the world has never seen. Human suffering would be immense.

It's not a pretty picture is it? Maybe we're closer to midnight than we think.

The United States, the most powerful nation in the world, is also struggling. Our own debt threatens our continued prosperity. We face the legitimate prospect that our children will suffer, perhaps greatly, for our continuing imprudent actions. Our morals are eroding. We need leaders who will act with selflessness, wisdom, integrity, and good stewardship. Passing legislation without reading it is a dereliction of duty especially when it affects a significant portion of the American economy and its citizens' way of life. Our government spending is out of control and defies all common sense. Individuals and institutions need to live within their means. The vast majority of our leaders do not recklessly spend money they do not have in their own households, so why should they spend the people's money in such a way? If they cannot grasp this fundamental concept, they are not qualified to lead.

Terrorist organizations and regimes driven by perverted religious ideology are hell bent on killing us. This threat is not to be understated. Our porous borders, especially our southern border, only enhance this threat. If our leaders do not grasp the magnitude of this danger, then they are unfit to govern.

These are just a few of the many complex problems that we face, and we intuitively seek elaborate solutions. A sophisticated solution is not the answer. We need to return to the basics—to the fundamental principles that made this country great. If we, the people, are flawed in our thoughts and actions, then our nation will be flawed as well. If the individual members of any sports team are executing improperly, then there is no way that the team can perform well. In such cases, the coach typically conducts a review of the fundamentals. As individuals and as a nation, we need to do the same. Defining the proper steps to take and the attitude to have are critical to getting this nation going in the right direction. Our nation is at a crossroads as we ponder which direction offers the greatest hope. Our ultimate hope however, rests not on what direction we follow, but on Whom.

We need to start at the top. We are a nation under God, and He is the One that we must follow. This is the most fundamental principle to grasp. Any step taken without God is a misstep. Physical action guided through wise insight is important, but proper spiritual alignment is imperative. If our spiritual alignment is correct, then the rest will naturally fall into place. Even true wisdom comes from God. "The fear of the LORD is the beginning of wisdom, and knowledge of the Holy One is understanding" (Proverbs 9:10 NIV). We cannot even start down the path of wisdom without first having reverence and respect toward God.

Does this mean that we all need to rush out and go to seminary? No, but increasing our faith and commitment to God are essential goals. The vast majority of us are not preachers, theologians, or Bible scholars. We don't wear the white collar of priesthood. We are "blue collar" in our walk of faith, and together, we make up the beautiful mosaic of the body of Christ. Some of us are hands; some are feet. Others are eyes, ears, or mouths. And yes, some are gall bladders or spleens that function entirely unseen. It doesn't matter what part you are. It only matters that you show up for work—to make yourself available for God's purposes.

Our primary action in daily life is to be salt and light in the world—adding flavor to life and providing an example to those around us. We do this by serving and encouraging others, and speaking the truth in love about the amazing saving grace of our Lord Jesus Christ. There is no higher honor than serving the Lord in whatever capacity you are called to serve Him. We are His children and are eternally blessed by this fact.

If we follow these basic concepts and principles both individually and as a nation, we will prosper. This is not anything new or revolutionary. This isn't the latest get-well-quick fad. These concepts have been with humankind for thousands of years and are built into our founding documents and Constitution. These four principles are:

1. We have a loving Creator of the universe Who desires a personal relationship with every human being on the planet. This is a love relationship between the Creator and His creations.
2. This relationship can be achieved only through His Son, Jesus Christ. To experience it, we must first accept Christ as our Lord and Savior. This monumental, life-changing event creates a new nature within ourselves and makes us adopted children of God and heirs to His kingdom.
3. The Bible is the inspired Word of God. It is His handbook for living life to its fullest and is useful for inspiration, teaching, rebuking, correcting, and training in righteousness. We should be doers of the Word. Every decision we make and action we take should be prefaced on this fundamental principle within our hearts: *God first.*
4. We are to be respectful of others and follow the Golden Rule: *Do unto others as you would want them to do unto you, and love them as you love yourself.*

An atheist or agnostic can at least follow the fourth principle, the Golden Rule. If we all simply followed that one rule, think of all the crime, hate, and human suffering we could eliminate. A non-Christian may also include the first principle. The absolute best approach is to follow all four. It is the ultimate way to live. We are children of God, and we have a perfect Father. He loves us more than anyone else does or ever could.

If we, the people, accept Christ as Lord and follow His teachings found in God's Word, then this nation will resolve its conflicts, heal its wounds, and be restored to great prosperity. Jesus is our only hope for the right kind of change. Any other answer is a destiny of destruction.

It's time to get ourselves right with God, and this process starts within our hearts. What we believe and prioritize will drive our actions and direct our decision-making. We need to get started now. There's not much time left—it's six minutes to midnight.

Are you spiritually ready for the midnight hour?

2. All the Wasted Time

Rick Saltzer

"So I guess I'm dying, huh?" she asked me with a tone of exhausted resignation. *Boom!* There it was: the question we had successfully avoided all day. My dad and brother had long been asleep upstairs, and it was well past 2:00 a.m. Now that we were alone and the house was completely quiet save for the ominous clicking of the oxygen machine, my mother apparently felt it was time to address the dreaded subject.

I, however, was not ready. Her frank query had caught me with my guard down; one minute, I was relaxed and reading the Bible to her, and the next, she had me pinned with the bluntest question imaginable.

Like a naughty child caught in a lie, I swallowed hard and quickly looked away. My mind raced for something soothing but substantial to say. The matter-of-fact manner in which Mom had asked the question unnerved me. It was as if she had been merely watching us and waiting for someone to have the guts to tell her what she already knew.

With much effort, I made myself look over at her on the bed, and I managed to mumble something rambling and stupid about the universal nature of death.

She said nothing, patiently waiting for her son to cease the pseudo-philosophy and answer her question. Her expression almost appeared to be one of pity for me in my obvious discomfort, rather than concern for herself and my response. When I had gathered my thoughts and was able to spit out what the oncologist had told us earlier that morning, she remained silent, but her face took on a remarkable look of relief and serenity. Seemingly satisfied by hearing the truth, she calmly leaned back on her pillow and asked me to continue reading to her from John.

After several minutes, I glanced up and saw that she was paying virtually no attention to me. I read on until I noticed that her eyes were darting rapidly and intently around the walls of the living room where we had set up her bed. It took me awhile to figure out that she was actually studying the family photographs that lined the tables and walls surrounding her.

Worried about this sudden change in her demeanor, I tried to interrupt her manic state by asking what she was thinking. Little did I know, at that point, the impact that her reply would have on my life.

Without looking at me and continuing to gaze at the familiar faces, she sighed and said, almost offhandedly, "All the wasted time…All the wasted time, and none of it even mattered."

That brief exchange turned out to be the last bit of lucid dialogue I ever had with Mom. She faded in and out of consciousness for the next three weeks or so and died early on a hot June morning with her three guys by her side, amidst a roomful of her best memories. She had accepted Christ as her Savior a few years prior to her illness, and she was prepared and ready to move on to Him. All she had needed to finally let go were a confirmation that her physical fight was over and a last chance to visually drink in the most significant images of her life.

However, Mom's unabashed deathbed observation never left me. The truth that she realized and shared with me in her last moments has served as the rock of wisdom around which I have attempted to live my life ever since. Though spoken indirectly, my mother's final advice to not waste time was the best gift she could have ever given me. I was taught my most valuable life lesson by a loved one experiencing death. Now it would be incumbent upon me to live my own life so as not to have similar regrets when God called me home.

As believers, most of us are familiar with many Bible verses related to the ideal use of our time: Eph. 5:15–17; Matt. 6:19–34/Luke 12:22–34; Luke 19:11–27; Matt. 22:36–40; and Eccles. 12:8–14, for example. We study and discuss these fundamental teachings in church and Sunday school our entire Christian lives. But how often and with what degree of regularity do we apply these truths in day-to-day living?

Here are some of the questions I was forced to ask myself after that long night with my mom:

- Did I know what was truly important in life? Did I know what was temporal versus eternal?
- Did I know what truly mattered in terms of eternity? Did I truly love others?
- Did I expend too much time fretting over things and events rather than using my time to serve others?
- Did I spend too much time on amusement/entertainment? Did I find myself "killing time?"
- Did I complicate my life unnecessarily with meaningless distractions?

In a nutshell, would I discipline myself to use the time that God had given me in a manner more pleasing to Him? Would I use my time more wisely so that I'd never have to reflect bitterly upon "all the wasted time" when my life was ending? Would I use her view of the past to alter my future?

Yes, I decided. *I will.*

And that decision to reset my priorities and redirect my time changed my life forever.

Thanks, Mom.

3. A Christian Nation

Although it is no longer in the forefront of the news, much debate was prompted by our president's comments in Turkey and elsewhere that the United States is not a Christian nation. It takes just a little investigation into the truth to discover that America was founded as a Christian nation, but the real question to its current citizenry is, "Does it really matter whether or not we remain one?" Americans' answer to this simple question and their subsequent actions will dramatically impact our nation's destiny.

Our country's first official document, the Declaration of Independence, refers to a Creator (God). Of that document's 56 signers, 29 held degrees in, or were formally educated in, theology. The first session of Congress began with three hours of worship during which five chapters of the Bible were read. The peace agreement signed between the United States and England after the Revolutionary War begins with the words, "In the name of the Most Holy Trinity." The first mass-printing of the Bible in America was authorized and funded by the U.S. Congress (worthwhile stimulus spending) to be read primarily in schools (worthwhile learning)...and the list goes on.[1] America's Declaration of Independence proclaims that we are a nation under God, and our very Constitution concludes by stating that it is signed "In the Year of Our Lord..."

To what Lord is this referring? Lord Cornwallis? Perhaps Lord Darth Vader? No. It is Jesus Christ, our Lord, and the "Our" means "our nation's" Lord. That sounds pretty Christian to me.

So how did we end up with the elected leader of our country stating that we are not a Christian nation? To be fair, our president must lead our *e pluribus unum* ("out of many, one") nation, and our Constitution promotes the freedom of worship for all religions. However, that does not require us to ignore or minimize our foundational Christian heritage. It seems we are sacrificing truth upon the altar of appeasement and political correctness. Some influential people today consider political correctness and the principles of humanism to be the apex of intellectual enlightenment, but in fact, truth is the apex of all enlightenment. If something is true, then it should be acknowledged. Denying or ignoring the truth never has beneficial consequences.

Jesus made an analogy during His ministry that He is the vine and we are the branches, implying a living dependence on Him (John 15:1). He also said, "I am the Way and the Truth and the Life. No one comes to the Father except through Me" (John 14:6 NIV). Every individual must ponder, and we as a nation must also decide, whether this is a true statement or a lie. One cannot be "sorta pregnant" about it. We cannot simply vote "present." We must choose.

The founding fathers overwhelmingly believed that this claim from Jesus is true and built this into our Constitution. He is the Rock upon which our Constitution stands. He is "our" Lord. It's now our turn to carry forward and reaffirm this truth or surrender it to either apathy or outright falsehood.

Thomas Jefferson, our third president, offered these words in prayer on behalf of our nation. His words reflect the spiritual emphasis embedded in our national consciousness and his petition to our Heavenly Father is as valid today as it was over 200 years ago:

> Almighty God, Who has given us this good land for our heritage; We humbly beseech Thee that we may always prove ourselves a people mindful of Thy favor and glad to do Thy will. Bless our land with honorable ministry, sound learning, and pure manners. Save us from violence, discord, and confusion, from pride and arrogance, and from every evil way. Defend our liberties, and fashion into one united people, the multitude brought hither out of many kindreds and tongues. Endow with Thy spirit of wisdom those whom in Thy name we entrust the authority of government, that there may be justice and peace at home, and that through obedience to Thy law, we may show forth Thy praise among the nations of the earth. In time of prosperity, fill our hearts with thankfulness, and in the day of trouble, suffer not our trust in Thee to fail; all of which we ask through Jesus Christ our Lord. Amen.
>
> — Washington D.C., March 4, 1801[2]

America faces many challenges today. We are embroiled in two wars, and our economy is struggling. We haven't had a balanced budget since 2001, and our deficit and debt continue to grow in dramatic fashion. This unrestrained spending will someday bankrupt our country. Denying our Christian heritage, however, will bankrupt our country's soul.

We rightly have separation of church and state—but not God and state. The church and the state are separate entities, but both are under God.

The whole universe is under God. The intent of any separation was not to protect the state from the church, but to protect the church from the state so that a president, once elected, could not declare that everyone must become a Presbyterian, a radical rattlesnake revivalist, or Yohimbe tree worshipper. We are free to worship as we choose. We are not a theocracy; our form of government is a republic, under God, with Jesus Christ as our Lord. That's how it was set up, and that's how it's supposed to be.

Thus, being a Christian nation does not mean dictating religion to its citizens or even to others, for Christians do not fear other beliefs. The commission of the Christian faithful is simply to be a light to others and through the good works of kindness, charity, and speaking the truth in love (not in arrogance or self-righteousness), truth and love will eventually prevail. Being a Christian nation is also not just about following Christian principles; although, if everyone in this nation were to practice them, then we would not have the crime, broken families, and financial mess that we currently face. Being a Christian nation is the official acknowledgement of an almighty God, the embracing of His Son, and the sharing of His love to the world. It is this foundational belief that through the "Vine" (Jesus), America (the branch) has incredibly prospered and produced such an abundance of fruit as to become the most generous and giving nation in the history of civilization.

We have not always acted perfectly. Sometimes our execution falls short of our ideals, but we were birthed as a Christian nation with the Trinity-Godhead as our inspiration, foundation, and source of our freedom. This is one truth that we dare not let slip away, for if we deny this truth, our requests that "God Bless America" will go unanswered. If we allow our leaders through thought, word, and deed (legislation and judicial rulings) to sever our country from the "Vine," the root source of our greatness, our destiny as a nation will be to wither and die.

4. Knock. Knock.

You never know when an opportunity will present itself. The saying "I'd rather be lucky than good" is amusing, but banking on random good fortune is a low-percentage bet. As a general principle, we should all follow the motto of the Boy and Girl Scouts: *Be Prepared.* Preparation enables us to recognize an opportunity and take advantage of it. Being lucky is more than simply being in the right place at the right time. Even if people are in a fortunate circumstance, if they don't recognize the opportunity or have failed to prepare themselves to take advantage of it, then that opportunity will slip away from them. In many cases, they won't even know that they missed it.

In the business world, experienced salespeople know this. There are often small windows of time when they have a chance to discuss their product or service to a potential customer. A good salesman will rehearse for this opportunity so that he is able to describe the features and benefits of his product or service in a short and concise manner. It's often called the "elevator pitch" as the duration is about the length of time of an elevator ride. It's rare that anyone can *close* a deal in such a short span, though closing is the ultimate goal. However, in this brief encounter, the initial objective is to plant enough seeds, pique enough curiosity, and provide enough interest that a follow up meeting can occur.

In our general walk in life, we are all salesmen. We communicate our ideas in persuasive speech; we present our opinions and thoughts to gain the acceptance of others, and we invite them to participate in our plans. Sometimes we "sell" passively by our actions and by how others interpret those actions.

Those of us who are Christians are all tasked to be salespeople. It's part of our job description as followers of Christ. Check it out:

> "Therefore, go and make disciples of all nations, baptizing them in the name of the Father and of the Son and of the Holy Spirit, and teaching them to obey everything I have commanded you. And surely I am with you always, to the very end of the age" (Matt. 28:19–20 NIV)
>
> But you will receive power when the Holy Spirit comes on you; and you will be My witnesses in Jerusalem, and in all Judea and Samaria, and to the ends of the earth (Acts 1:8 NIV).

Jesus' words in the verses above are referred to as the Great Commission. They were the last words that He spoke to His followers before He ascended into Heaven. It's not the Great Suggestion. When the Son of God says to do something, it's a command.

We need to be good Scouts and be prepared to witness to others. Create and rehearse your elevator pitch. Think of why you put your trust in Jesus, and be able to explain it in a simple way. This will accomplish two things: First, it confirms your own beliefs and arranges them into a logical and persuasive order, which should strengthen your own faith. Second, it enables you to give a confident answer to the questioner, which should further elevate his or her interest.

Even though Peter was a simple fisherman, he understood this. He wrote, "But in your hearts set apart Christ as Lord. Always be prepared to give an answer to everyone who asks you to give the reason for the hope that you have. But do this with gentleness and respect" (1 Pet. 3:15 NIV). The Apostle Paul offers similar advice, "Let your conversation be always full of grace, seasoned with salt, so that you may know how to answer everyone" (Col. 4:6 NIV).

Many are uncomfortable discussing their faith. You might be afraid that you won't give the right answers, or you may be afraid of what people will ask, or how they will respond. Just speak the truth in love (gentleness and respect) from your heart, and let the Holy Spirit speak through you. He will guide you. Start with your "elevator pitch" and let it flow from there. If the conversation gets difficult, then suggest a follow-up meeting where you can bring another witness, or simply invite them to church where they can request a meeting with one of the church staff.

Also, remember that what you do is at least as important as what you say. You can be a successful salesperson without saying a word—just let your actions speak for you. As Jesus said in the Sermon on the Mount: "Let your light shine before men in such a way that they may see your good works, and glorify your Father who is in Heaven" (Matt. 5:16 NASB). People observe what you do and how you act. Make sure you behave "in such a way" that brings glory to God—that you honor Him with righteous living, simply loving and treating others as well as you would treat yourself, and loving God with all you've got.

Actions speak louder than words, but be prepared for the opportunity to witness to those who may come and ask why you are the way you are. Have your elevator pitch at the ready to explain why you believe the way you believe. It may be just a planting of the seed, which someone else may water and another harvest—or it might be harvest time right then. Then you can be a chosen vessel of God to lead another soul to the Lord. Now, how cool is that? To close a deal for Christ.

5. Lost

Have you ever been lost? Or worse, lost and alone? I'm not talking about not being able to find someone's house or a restaurant when you're just a few blocks off and too stubborn to stop and ask directions. (Pride can be *such* an impediment to success.) No, I'm referring to a situation where you don't have a clue as to where you are or whether the direction you are currently traveling is any improvement upon your current predicament. It's not a good feeling is it?

I once got lost as a small child while our family was camping down in Florida. It wasn't a fun moment. Through retrospective rationalization, I've determined that it was really my sister's fault. When I was growing up, our family did a lot of camping. Mom and Dad would load up us kids in our camper and take us somewhere, and in this case, it was Florida. We were in a large campground with hundreds of campers, RVs, and trailers. A trading post stood near the center of the campground. One night, my older sister and I walked to this general store, and I saw some Batman cards. Like most six-year-olds, I wanted them. Now these weren't the *Dark Knight* Batman cards of today. These were the more cartoonish Batman and Robin, who fought bad guys with the "POW," "WHAM," and "ZOWEE" type of thing—more appropriate for a small youngster. My sister kept teasing me that she was not going to buy them for me.

All of you "babies" of the family out there know that it's a tough life being the youngest. So like any respectable, rebellious, recent graduate of kindergarten who was determined to get what he wanted, I ran out of the store to find my mom or dad and plead my case up the chain of command.

And I got lost.

I wandered up and down several roads for a few hours in the dark, crying and totally confused as to where I was. My parents, along with a few camping neighbors, set out to find me. Mom was worried that I might get run over or bitten by a snake. One of the fellow campers said that this probably wouldn't happen, but two dogs had gone missing over the past week, and they thought an alligator had gotten them. (Nothing like positive words of encouragement to help alleviate the stress of a worried mother.)

Finally, a fellow camper found me and took me to my campsite. My parents were greatly relieved to find me. Then, once I was safe, the judgment came. That was the only time my dad took off his belt and gave me a whipping. To complete this father-son endearing moment, my dad even told me that old cliché, "Son, this is going to hurt me more than it does you."

I sobbed in response, "Then why aren't you crying?" You know, sometimes it is best in situations like that just to be quiet and take your licking. Later, my sister did buy me the Batman cards. Somehow, they had lost their luster and appeal after that ordeal—a negative return-on-investment as the gain was well below the cost.

Despite that traumatic experience, being physically lost pales in comparison to being spiritually lost. In fact there is no comparison—none whatsoever. There is no more appropriate use of the warning, "Don't go there!"

Ponder this seriously for a moment. There is nothing of more importance for you to consider. If there is a God, the Creator of the universe, and if this Creator has established for us a life after this one that has far greater potential in terms of duration (eternity) and fulfillment (joy/peace/paradise) than this life, and if what you say, think, do, and believe in this life somehow affects the outcome or the status of your next life, then how should you live your life?

Well, holy perpetuity pontification Batman. Is this the ultimate riddle from the Riddler for us to consider?

Let's break this down in terms of return-on-investment (ROI). If there exists a future life after this earthly life that just knocks the socks slap off your feet, and it, like the Energizer Bunny, keeps going and going in a perfectly pleasing and particularly pleasurable manner, then how can you even quantify love, joy, and peace for all eternity? It goes right off the chart.

This is truly a no-brainer (but keep your brain, as you need it to read further). The simple answer is to say, think, do, and believe whatever it is that pleases the Creator. He's the One giving out the brownie points. *Duh.* Your payback is incalculable. Think about it. Even in the worst possible scenario, this is an awesome deal.

Let's consider the worst-case scenario. Here's an analogy. Perhaps you've seen the television show, *Dirty Jobs.* It portrays all sorts of undesirable occupations from the slightly unappealing to the grotesquely nasty. Let's say you've become a contestant who has to perform the worst possible job in the world; dream up your worst. You must work this job for an entire month, and to make it even more miserable, your living conditions during that month are equivalent to those experienced by the poorest of the poor.

After that one month, however, you get to retire in a mansion on a wonderful beach where you will live in luxury for the rest of your life. Would you take on such a challenge? What if how hard you worked during your month would determine what extra benefits and privileges you would get in retirement? Would you work your hardest? Of course, you would—or you should. What's one month compared to the rest of your life? In the grander, real-life scheme, what's a lifetime, even if you live to be 200 years old, compared to 2 trillion years? It's less than a rounding error.

Well, that's the deal. Our Heavenly Father has promised us a life with Him for all eternity. It is a place with many mansions and there is no pain, no suffering, and no tears except perhaps tears of joy and amazement at His abounding grace.

God is love (1 John 4:8), and His love surpasses human understanding. Think about a time when you were in love and felt love from another—I mean, truly felt the love. That is so miniscule compared to the love you will receive in Heaven that it doesn't even register on the scale. If all 7 billion people on planet earth simultaneously loved you with all their hearts, this would not come close to the immeasurable love our Heavenly Father has for you. Imagine being in an environment where you are surrounded by such love—all the time—for all eternity. That's what awaits those whose names are found written in the Book of Life. What a deal! It would require surgery to remove the smiles from our faces. In fact, it will be so wonderful that we will probably just childishly giggle with glee through the first 10,000 years.

So where do you sign up? All you must do is believe in the name of Christ Jesus and accept Him as your Lord and Savior. That's it. As for the extra benefits, well, that depends on your good works. God judges that, not necessarily by the outcomes, but by your attitude of heart. Let's go back to this belief gig, though, as it is the critical piece. The rest is just gravy. As you grow in faith, it will come through the Holy Spirit that resides in you.

The word "belief" in the English language is a bit watered down, as it implies a simple intellectual acceptance. True belief compels one to action. Let's say you are sitting alone on the couch watching your favorite TV show. It's an enjoyable show, and you're in full compliance with Newton's first law of motion—"A body at rest will remain at rest." (This is the mantra of couch potatoes.) Suddenly, you *believe* that you'll have something to drink. Well, it's not true belief unless you override Newton's law and get off the couch to get a drink. A more-heated example is that if you believed your hair was on fire, you wouldn't just sit there and let it burn—you'd try to put it out. Belief compels action.

Likewise, if you truly believe in God and His Son, it will change you and your way of living in all that you say, think, do, and believe because your whole perspective on how the universe operates is changed. Your priorities and internal governing rules of living life change. You will no longer walk in ignorance of God or in defiance of Him. You will not timidly cling to a false hope that maybe, just maybe, you have behaved good enough to receive a reward in the afterlife. When you accept Christ as your Lord, you will *know* that you are God's child. The Gospel means *good news*, and the good news is that God loves us and has offered His Son to pay for our sins so that those who trust in Him can spend the rest of eternity with Him in paradise. It's not just the best deal in town. It's the best deal in the universe! We should be shouting in the streets and telling everyone we know.

Now there is a flip side. It's not a catch; it's not in the small print—the print's the same size throughout the Bible. You can choose to reject this deal of a lifetime, and if you do, you're toast—burnt toast.

It's really not a joking matter—this is the most awful thing you could ever imagine. Think of a time when you were in pain—back pain, toothache, or worse. Consider a time when you were very anxious and felt hopeless about a situation. Now magnify both of those several thousand times into a constant, continuous state of suffering. That's a gruesome thought isn't it? Now here's the real kicker. However bad that is, and it's real bad, the killer is that there is no hope of it ever improving—ever. It is hopeless suffering for all eternity: the complete absence of hope. It is the blackest of the black, the worst of the worst, and more horrible than anything imaginable. You are lost—forever.

God provides us a simple choice to make—be with Him or without Him—and the consequences of our choice are beyond words. Nothing on Planet Earth is even remotely enticing enough for us to choose to be without Him. Even the best possible outcome without Christ is still a total loss. Jesus presented that ROI scenario quite plainly: "For what does it profit a man to gain the whole world, and forfeit his soul?" (Mark 8:36 NASB).

Don't be the ultimate loser. Get on the winning team and get a life with Christ.

6. Who Dat?

Say, who dat? Who dat, who? Who dat messin' with de mighty, mighty devils?

That was one of our cheers for our high school basketball team, along with, "You fouled my man. Hey boy, what's wrong with your head?" Perhaps in this stifling age of political correctness, such cheers would be considered inappropriate now. But our team, the mighty, mighty Red Devils of Graham High School in Graham, North Carolina, went undefeated that year in 1976 and won the state 3A basketball championship.

You can't knock perfection. In the end, every 3A school in the state knew who we were.

Sometimes it's important to know who someone is, and it's always important to know who you are. If you don't know who you are, there are shelves upon shelves of books written to help you find yourself, find your inner self, discover things about yourself, love yourself, and maximize your potential. In fact, someone somewhere has written something about almost anything you wanted to know about yourself, but were afraid to ask.

Going back to our mighty, mighty Red Devils high school, a mural was painted on the cafeteria walls with the proclamation that you are what you eat. Judging by some of the food served there, as in many school cafeterias, it was a scary thought.

Although food plays an important role in what we grow up to be (especially physically), a more encompassing assertion is to state that you are the sum total of the decisions that you make. That's an accurate statement isn't it? You are where you are today because of the decisions you made along the way—what car to drive, what house to buy, what food to eat, what job to take, what principles to follow, what precepts to believe, what person to marry. *Voila. Vous etes ici.* (You are here).

Pastor Andy Stanley of North Point Community Church in Atlanta, Georgia, wrote an insightful book about this concept entitled, *The Principle of the Path.* Where you end up in large part is due to the cumulative decisions you make along the way. Yes, sometimes events occur well outside our control that dramatically affect our lives, but the greatest influence of why you are where you are is determined by the decisions you have made. Your intentions mattered not, as the adage states that even the road to hell is paved with good intentions. It's your steps that matter, and it is best in this journey through life that we be wise in how we take our steps.

Though we are the cumulative sum of the choices we make, the vast majority of these decisions have negligible effect on where we are in life. Pondering what flavored gum to buy or what section of the newspaper to read first rarely alters the course of human history. There are, however, a few choices and one decision in particular that have a huge impact on who we become and where we end up.

Mark records in his gospel (8:27–29) something that occurred while Jesus was traveling along with His disciples to villages around Caesarea Philippi. [The story is also told in the other two Synoptic Gospels (see Matt. 16:13 and Luke 9:18)]. While they are strolling along, Jesus (perhaps casually) asks His disciples, "Who do people say that I am?" (ESV).

They answer Him, "John the Baptist; and others say Elijah; but others, one of the prophets" (ESV).

Then, I envision Jesus just stopping right there in the middle of the road for a dramatic pause as His disciples gather around Him. They know He is about to say something important. Slowly scanning their faces and looking intently into their eyes, Jesus asks them, "But who do you say that I am?"

This question, folks, is a biggie. And it's not just meant for the disciples; it is for every human being on Planet Earth.

Your answer and subsequent actions inspired by your answer is more important than what house you buy, what career you have, or what person you marry. This has eternal consequences: forever-and-ever-type stuff.

So let's pause for a moment to consider it very carefully. What's the real deal with this Jewish carpenter that lived in Palestine 2,000 years ago?

First of all, no matter what you believe, you must objectively admit that no person in human history has had a greater impact on mankind than Jesus of Nazareth. Who even comes close? Here is a man who the entire world bases its calendar by the estimated date of His birth. He performed incredible miracles, taught an amazing philosophy and approach to living a life with abundance, and after being crucified, rose from the dead! These events were all predicted by Jewish prophets—some over a 1,000 years before they were fulfilled. Professor Emeritus of Science at Westmont College Peter Stoner, along with 600 of his students, calculated the probability of one person fulfilling just eight of the Biblical prophecies (found in Micah 5:2, Mal. 3:1, Zech. 9:9, Zech. 13:6, Zech. 11:2, Zech. 11:13, Isa. 53:7, and Ps. 22:16) was 1 in 100,000,000,000,000,000.[1] Most Bibles list over forty prophecies fulfilled by Jesus, and some scholars claim the number of prophecies fulfilled by Christ exceed 400. I think we can say with a high degree of confidence that we have our man. Today, nearly a third of the entire world considers Him to be the Son of God, and well, He either is, or he is not. It's one of those decisions that you can't be ambivalent about or simply take a pass.

Though other religions may refer to Jesus as a holy man, a prophet, a miracle worker, or a human who achieved some New Age godlike qualities, this is wholly inadequate to what He claimed. That's worse than calling the president of the United States just a civil servant. Jesus claimed to be the Son of God: "I and the Father are One" (John 10:30); "Before Abraham was, I AM" (John 8:58); "I am the living bread that came down from Heaven" (John 6:51); "If you've seen Me, you've seen the Father" (John 14:9); to name just a few examples. To put it quite bluntly, He is either telling the truth or a lie. It's the ultimate *Ripley's Believe It or Not.* There is no in-between.

There are only three possibilities for Jesus—one of three Ls. He is either a liar by claiming to be the Son of God when he is not, a lunatic in that he thought he was the Son of God, but was mistaken, or He is the Legitimate Son of God Who sits at the right hand of the Father and will someday come to judge the living and the dead.

Once again this logic goes against political correctness as truth typically does. The only way that Jesus could be a holy man, a prophet, or a good teacher is if He truly were the Son of God. For a holy man, a prophet, or a good teacher cannot lie, nor can they be insane. A legitimate prophet can only speak the truth. Jesus claimed to be the Son of God, so in order for Him to be a holy man or a prophet, He must be telling the truth. This then elevates Him above simply being a holy man or prophet to His rightful place as the Son of God sitting at the right hand of the Father. It is this belief that Jesus is the Christ, the Messiah, and the Son of God upon which the entire Christian faith hangs. This faith is either completely right or completely wrong—there's no partial credit or consolation prize for playing.

Considering all the facts, it is difficult to imagine how anyone could conclude that Jesus Christ is a lunatic or a liar. To think such is foul. *(Hey boy, what's wrong with your head?)* No one would willingly go through scourging and the horrific torture of crucifixion to promote a lie.

No one crazy could speak such wisdom and perform such miracles. God would not honor a fool through resurrection.

Just examine the subsequent actions of the disciples. They ran in fear when Jesus was captured. Then after seeing the resurrected Lord, they boldly went forth proclaiming the Gospel message that Jesus Christ is Lord and the Savior of the world. For these actions, most of them were martyred. They lived beyond faith—they lived in fact as firsthand witnesses of the risen Lord. They all experienced personally the response given by Thomas, the one who doubted Jesus' resurrection until he directly put his finger in the nail holes in Jesus' hands and his hand in the wound in Jesus' side. When he did this, there was only one reply possible: "My Lord and my God." (John 20:28 NASB).

What's interesting to note is the dialogue between Jesus and Thomas during this special encounter. Jesus did not admonish Thomas for his lack of faith. He didn't smack him on top of the head and say, "Whatsamatter with you? I've been with you for three years. Didn't you listen to what I was saying?" No, Jesus simply responded, "Because you have seen Me, you have believed; blessed are those who have not seen and yet have believed" (John 20:29 NASB).

Jesus did not criticize Thomas for his doubt. He did however pronounce a blessing to all those who come to Christ in faith, especially to those who arrive there without the unique privilege that Thomas had of seeing Christ for himself.

So where are you in your assessment of Jesus Christ? Are you full of doubt? Is He a liar, a lunatic, or Lord of your life? If you're still unsure, just ask Him. Jesus is not troubled by your doubt and fears. Earnestly seek Him. Call to Him with true sincerity in prayer and ask Him to reveal Himself to you. He is already knocking at the door of your heart. Ask Him to come on in.

When you do, your life will change forever. You will know who Jesus is and will agree that there is only one correct answer. Peter gave it when he said, "You are the Christ, the Son of the living God" (Matt. 16:16 NASB).

Don't be messing with dat devil. Get in on the winning team with God's Son. He is "Our Lord and our God," and you can take that truth to the spiritual bank. Believe on it and be saved.

7. One Way

You may have heard the saying, "There's more than one way to skin a cat." In order to achieve PETA-approved political correctness, I guess I should have chosen another phrase, but that was the first adage to come to mind, and it fits. Actually, I think the reference to "cat" refers to a catfish, so since there's no fur involved, perhaps they won't mind.

Anyway, it means that there is more than one way to do something. In the military, we used to say that there was a right way, a wrong way, and the military way, which was always somewhere in between. Here's one unofficial navy slogan: *The Navy: over 200 years of tradition unmarred by progress.*

In professional consulting, the term *best practices* is repeated almost ad nauseam. That's the purpose of a consultant, however: they are subject-matter experts on their particular endeavor and have to be able to complete a task or set of tasks in not just any way, but in the best way possible—typically in terms of quality, cost, and speed.

In travel, there always seem to be multiple ways to get to a place. Any GPS unit can calculate multiple routes for you based on preprogrammed priorities such as shortest driving distance or maximizing the use of interstate highways.

In the spiritual realm, are there many paths to God? If all roads lead to Rome, then do all paths lead to God? Is there a "best practices" path—one that is simply better than the others? Perhaps it is a blended solution where each faith has some things right and some things wrong, so if you piece all the right stuff together in the right way, then you'll have the grand answer—the spiritual equivalent of a World Religion *Greatest Hits* CD? These are important points to ponder.

If we follow this culture's obsession with political correctness, then the answer must be "yes" to the multiple-paths-to-God question. It would be politically incorrect to say otherwise. It doesn't take much scholarly analysis, however, to recognize that this is impossible. Some religions say that there is only one God, while others proclaim many gods ranging from a few to over a million. *Somebody* has miscounted. Some faiths promote the idea of a unique soul belonging to each individual while others promote a recycled soul (reincarnation). Both of these beliefs may be wrong, but both cannot be right–if one is correct, the other must be wrong. Some faiths promote an afterlife while others do not. Of those that support some type of afterlife, all but Christianity believe that some method of measuring people's good works versus their bad determines their final destination in this next life. Christianity claims that all of us are unworthy of heaven, but that faith in Christ *makes* us worthy, and is the only road to salvation. The deeper you go, the more incompatible the various faiths become. Most are outright mutually exclusive of each other. In other words, believing in one faith makes believing in another faith impossible. There may, in fact, be many paths to God, but it seems that all but one must have a Bridge Out Ahead sign somewhere along the way. In the final analysis, political correctness in religion is a lie.

So what is true? What is the one right path to God? We get to choose what we believe, but that choice shouldn't be based on our whims, family upbringing, or what best fits our desired lifestyle. It should be based on the truth, and it's incumbent upon all of us to seek that truth with all our heart. You have the Talmud, the Koran, Buddha's Seven Noble Truths, the Bible, and others to explore. Investigate them all if you are unsure, for it is incredibly important that you choose the right path. No one wants to go down a road to God only to discover that its bridge is out and you fall into Monty Python's "gorge of eternal peril."

All things equal, the "best practices" recommendation would be to start with Christianity, as it not only has the largest number of followers, but virtually all the other religions view the Christian Savior, Jesus Christ, as at least a holy man or prophet. This streamlines your investigation efforts in terms of quality, cost, and speed. The crux of the matter quickly becomes, "Is Jesus just a holy man or prophet no different than Moses, Buddha, Mohammed, or any other celebrated religious figure? Or is He the Son of God?"

The Bible is quite clear on Whom Jesus is and what is the correct road to salvation. There is no ambiguity or an allusion to an alternate back road. There is only one path. We have a Creator Who desires a relationship with us. He loves us so incredibly much that He wants us to address Him as Father. He wants us to know His Son, and He makes it very clear through His inspired Word that His Son is the Way to Him:

> "But as many as received Him, to them He gave the right to become children of God, even to those who believe in His name" (John 1:12 NASB).
>
> "Whoever believes in the Son has eternal life, but whoever rejects the Son will not see life, for God's wrath remains on him" (John 3:36 NIV).
>
> "You search the Scriptures because you think that in them you have eternal life; it is these that testify about Me; and you are unwilling to come to Me so that you may have life" (John 5:39–40 NASB).
>
> "I tell you the truth, he who believes has everlasting life" (John 6:47 NIV).
>
> "I am the door; if anyone enters through Me, he will be saved, and will go in and out and find pasture" (John 10:9 NASB).

"Jesus said to her, 'I am the resurrection and the life; he who believes in Me will live even if he dies, and everyone who lives and believes in Me will never die. Do you believe this?'" (John 11:25–26 NASB).

"Jesus did many other miraculous signs in the presence of His disciples, which are not recorded in this book. But these are written that you may believe that Jesus is the Christ, the Son of God, and that by believing you may have life in His name" (John 20:30–31 NIV).

"And there is salvation in no one else; for there is no other name under Heaven that has been given among men by which we must be saved" (Acts 4:12 NASB).

"Of Him all the prophets bear witness that through His name everyone who believes in Him receives forgiveness of sins" (Acts 10:43 NASB).

"We believe that we are all saved the same way, by the undeserved grace of the Lord Jesus" (Acts 15:11 NLT).

"They replied, 'Believe in the Lord Jesus, and you will be saved—you and your household'" (Acts 16:31 NIV).

"In Him we have redemption through His blood, the forgiveness of our trespasses, according to the riches of His grace" (Eph. 1:7 ESV).

"And the testimony is this, that God has given us eternal life, and this life is in His Son. He who has the Son has the life; he who does not have the Son of God does not have the life. These things I have written to you who believe in the name of the Son of God, so that you may know that you have eternal life" (1 John 5:11–13 NASB).

"For I am not ashamed of this Good News about Christ. It is the power of God at work, saving everyone who believes—the Jew first and also the Gentile" (Rom. 1:16 NLT).

"For the wages of sin is death, but the gift of God is eternal life in Christ Jesus our Lord" (Rom. 6:23 NIV).

"Whoever will call on the name of the Lord will be saved" (Rom. 10:13 NASB).

"Now, brothers, I want to remind you of the gospel I preached to you, which you received and on which you have taken your stand. By this gospel you are saved, if you hold firmly to the word I preached to you. Otherwise, you have believed in vain. For what I received I passed on to you as of first importance: that Christ died for our sins according to the Scriptures" (1 Cor. 15:1–3 NIV).

"Jesus gave His life for our sins, just as God our Father planned, in order to rescue us from this evil world in which we live" (Gal. 1:4 NLT).

"I am shocked that you are turning away so soon from God, who called you to Himself through the loving mercy of Christ. You are following a different way that pretends to be the Good News but is not the Good News at all. You are being fooled by those who deliberately twist the truth concerning Christ. But even if we or an angel from Heaven should preach a gospel other than the one we preached to you, let him be eternally condemned" (Gal. 1:6–8 NLT).

"You are all sons of God through faith in Christ Jesus" (Gal. 3:26 NIV).

"This is a trustworthy saying, and everyone should accept it: 'Christ Jesus came into the world to save sinners'—and I am the worst of them all" (1 Tim. 1:15 NLT).

"For there is one God and one mediator between God and men, the man Christ Jesus" (1 Tim. 2:5 NIV).

"And from Jesus Christ, the faithful witness, the firstborn of the dead, and the ruler of the kings of the earth. To Him who loves us and released us from our sins by His blood" (Rev. 1:5 NIV).

> "Blessed be the God and Father of our Lord Jesus Christ, Who according to His great mercy has caused us to be born again to a living hope through the resurrection of Jesus Christ from the dead, to obtain an inheritance which is imperishable and undefiled and will not fade away, reserved in Heaven for you" (1 Peter 1:3–4 NASB).

The Bible is a love story about the Creator in continual pursuit of His created. Our Heavenly Father loves us and desires that no one should perish, but that all receive eternal life. He has provided through inspiration over 400 verses (according to Dr. Jack Van Impe's count, and he can probably recite them all) of Scripture that tell us exactly how. "How do I love thee? Let me count the ways." Here's the main one:

> "For God so loved the world that He gave His only begotten Son, that whoever believes in Him shall not perish, but have eternal life" (John 3:16 NASB).

This is an incredible act of love that God the Father would sacrifice His Son in order to have a relationship with us. Now think logically about this for a moment and consider this hypothetical scenario. Let's say you were a parent of a child with a special characteristic and suddenly the entire world was inflicted with a deadly virus. All of humankind would die in a matter of weeks, and the only cure was something absolutely unique in your child's blood that could produce a vaccine that would save the planet. In order to produce this vaccine, your child had to die. Now how's that for a parental dilemma? To save the human race, you must sacrifice your child.

Would you do it?

You certainly wouldn't even consider it if there was another way. Do you think that God, all-knowing and all-loving, would have sacrificed

His Son if there were an alternative method? Would Jesus surrender His life for our sakes if there was a backdoor route into salvation? He even prayed fervently, sweating blood, asking the Father if there was another way. There was no other way. If there was, then Jesus' sacrificial death on the cross would not have been required. Even within our limited intellectual capacity, we should easily grasp this logical truth.

Do you want to know the one way, the only way to God? "Jesus answered, 'I am the Way and the Truth and the Life. No one comes to the Father except through Me'" (John 14:6 NIV). There is no bridge out on His path. He is the road to the Father; He is the way to life eternal. When you travel with Jesus, you will always get to the right destination.

8. Facing Our Fears

Doug Hanson

It was late September 2004 when I made my return visit to Reghin, Romania, to visit with Oana Frandes's family. I had met Oana one year before on a flight from Atlanta, and she became a most valuable translator for research into the whereabouts of orphans displaced from the Walk in the Light orphanage across northern Romania. Her mother, Maria, was kind enough to put me up in her Communist apartment near the town square and had prepared the living room couch for my bedding prior to my visit.

The next morning dawned beautifully crisp with a fresh wind down from the Ukraine and clear blue skies. Oana wanted me to see the local orphanage of twenty children sponsored by a UK philanthropic organization that was also near the square. For several years, Oana had volunteered there, caring for the kids and building solid relationships. Following general introductions to the staff and most of the kids, Oana suggested that we paint all of the kids' faces using the stamping method because of the large numbers. Volunteering as the guinea pig, Oana asked for a spider and the manager asked for a butterfly on her cheek. When they were both finished, all of the kids wanted their choices. They waited in line for almost an hour before we completed the entire group.

With this success behind us, and the noon hour approaching, Oana and I moved to the central park to set up a painting site on a concrete bench. We looked for kids to paint and bring some joy to their day. Business was slow, so Oana opted to put on a bright gold metallic wig and walked over to the nearby swings to round-up some early volunteers. She had little trouble in getting a group together, and soon I was painting numbers of kids. Each had selected their styles from books that I had brought for them to peruse.

After six or seven kids had their entire faces painted and they dispersed throughout the park, more and more kids became intrigued with the free offering. Oana was most patient in translating to me their preferences, and the kids and their parents delighted in the unusual opportunity.

After a few more were painted, a couple and their young son, who looked about six, slowly approached our painting venue. The young boy was crying, and the parents were busy consoling him. It turned out the boy had been sitting in a dentist chair in a nearby third floor office building near the park and he became frightened with the prospect of a tooth extraction. In Romania, dentists do not use Novocain, and children are petrified when they think about having their teeth pulled. The boy's parents had suggested a walk in the park to settle the youngster down. They saw the commotion around our face paintings and approached the area with interest.

I asked the little boy what he wanted to do. He said he "wanted to scare the dentist, because he had scared him." "Fair enough." I said. "What would you like your face to be?" I asked. He replied, "A tigre," which is Romanian for tiger.

With great confidence, the little guy brightened, straddled the concrete bench, and faced me for the white, yellow, and orange base coat. Then, after a few minutes of drying time, I painted the outline of the eyes, the nose, and whiskers, and he was finished. When he saw his face in a hand mirror, he exclaimed, "Let's go." His confidence had returned, and he was ready to scare his dentist.

At least forty minutes passed as numerous other boys and girls came for their personal makeover. Laughter and joy abounded as the kids looked at one another and enjoyed the moment. Oana gave instructions on how to clean and wash up the paints, and excitedly, the kids kept scouting for more of their friends to join in their fun.

It was then that I looked down the long, pebbled gravel path to see one of my painted faces approaching our area. It was the little guy coming from his successful dental appointment holding the hands of both his parents. He had told his parents that he wanted to return to me to give me a hug and thank me for giving him this new courage to frighten his dentist and endure the pain from the extraction.

I was almost in tears as I hugged the little guy. I took a moment to contemplate the situation: Here I was halfway around the world in a country where I did not know the language providing a skill that few children had ever experienced. I had no signs for advertising and took no pay for services. I was there in Reghin for this one little guy, who without his tiger "face" of courage, would have had a frightening experience in the dental chair. It was a moment in time orchestrated by God to use me in a most unexpected way to make the difference in this little man's day—and perhaps his life and many others who braved their fears to approach this American visitor.

Oana—she could not contain her joy as we left the park after spending three hours with the kids. It was a day she too would never forget.

9. Priority Check

Rick Saltzer

I had a plan for Saturday:
to complete a large to-do list –
a day for work and not for play,
I plunged in while pumping my fist

Sweat was dripping all over me
when I noticed my little boy
smiling at me excitedly,
as if he had found a new toy

I'm sure I looked sort of confused
as we knelt there out on the lawn –
I asked why he seemed so enthused –
it was then I finally caught on

I'd promised since last September
that "tomorrow" we would play ball –
I didn't think he would remember,
but this time he chose to recall

It was clear that I'd forgotten
        and had borne out my son's worst fears –
I stood there feeling plain rotten,
        watching his eyes filling with tears

As I worked, his eyes grew wetter,
        and even more so when I asked,
"Wouldn't tomorrow be better?" –
        and then I was fully unmasked

He stopped sobbing out of sheer pride,
        and fought to restrain his sorrow –
then he wiped his nose and replied,
        "Daddy, today *is* tomorrow" –

10. Give It Up.

My great-grandfather, Harvey Caswell McAllister, served as a first lieutenant in the North Carolina 8th Regiment, Company H, in the War Between the States. Most history books refer to it as the American Civil War. Southerners refer to it as the War of Northern Aggression. He was a farmer, but he didn't own any slaves—he had nine kids instead. After the war, Harvey went into contracting and built the Lutheran church in Mount Pleasant, North Carolina, which still stands today. He served a couple of terms as a state legislator. There was nothing extravagant or flashy about my great-grandfather's life—just your good old-fashioned salt and light in the world.

As one of his descendants and part of the elect ("American by birth and Southern by the Grace of God"), I am absolutely galled to quote a Yankee general (a cigar-chomping, drunk one at that), whose soldiers were responsible for wounding ole Harvey twice (one in the knee, the other in the thigh) during the siege of Petersburg. Unfortunately, there are no more appropriate words to describe the attitude with which we should approach our Heavenly Father than the ones Gen. Ulysses. S. Grant used in the capture of Fort Donelson:

Unconditional Surrender.

These words are even hard for me to type. They certainly don't roll easily off my tongue. There's something inside every human being—and not just those of Southern heritage—that makes it distasteful to us to give in. Perseverance is an excellent and Godly trait. James, the Lord's brother tells us to "let our perseverance grow, for when your endurance is fully developed, you will be perfect and complete, needing nothing" (James 1:4 NLT). The key is in the source of the motivation. Are we motivated to serve God or serve ourselves? It's been commented upon for decades, but we are still deep into the evolution of the "Me Generation." It's all about us. We perceive everything from our myopic point of view—from the most important to the mundane. Our dedication is primarily egocentrically driven.

Ever been in a group photo? Who's the first person you look for? It's not "Look at Fred acting crazy." or "What's up with Suzy's hair?" Those comments may come later, but the first thing you look for is you. We're hardwired that way. It's part of our fallen state. Our greatest interest is ourselves.

In his bestseller, *The 7 Habits of Highly Effective People,* Stephen Covey teaches that we all act based on our "centers." We are all centered on something (our work, our money, our relationships, ourselves, etc.), Covey argues, that we will be happiest and most successful if we become *principle-centered* in our behavior.

Principles are a great start. Principles are like scientific laws. They are timeless in their application, universal in scope, and consistent in their results. They are not subject to the fickleness of emotions or the environment. If we choose Biblical principles, that's even better. God built this universe so He knows best how it operates. But the best alternative is to become *God-centered.*

Trying to manage our behavior by following a great set of principles means that we are still depending upon our own abilities to execute properly. The objective is correct, but it remains centered on our own efforts to get there. We must put God at the top as our highest priority and place Christ in the center of our hearts. We then surrender or submit our lives to Him. It's not about us—it's all about Him. It is a total trust, a total commitment, and a total surrender to Him. It's investing all you got. When you surrender all to God, He will live through you, guide you, and direct you to places and accomplishments that you could never imagine.

When you accept Jesus Christ as your Savior, you become a new you—not a rebuilt you, but a whole new person and nature. ("Therefore, if anyone is in Christ, he is a new creation; the old has gone, the new has come." 2 Cor. 5:17 NIV.) You are made completely righteous in God's eyes. That's great news. So what do we do with that? Well, we march out in our new nature trying to be good, and we fail. We try again, and we fail. We pray. We fast...and we fail some more. What's up with this? Even the mighty Apostle Paul, author of half the New Testament, expressed in frustration:

> "I want to do what is good, but I don't. I don't want to do what is wrong, but I do it anyway. But if I do what I don't want to do, I am not really the one doing wrong; it is sin living in me that does it. I have discovered this principle of life—that when I want to do what is right, I inevitably do what is wrong. I love God's law with all my heart. But there is another power within me that is at war with my mind. This power makes me a slave to the sin that is still within me. Oh, what a miserable person I am. Who will free me from this life that is dominated by sin and death?" (Rom. 7:19–24 NLT).

His answer is in verse 25: "Thank God. The answer is in Jesus Christ our Lord" (NLT).

Our problem is that we focus on our *behavior* and not on our *belief.* Behavior is driven by belief. In Bible lingo, belief begets behavior. So we need to focus our hearts on the Source. This is a heart and belief thing, not a muscle and do thing. Christ has already done all the work on the cross. Therefore, there is now no condemnation for those who are in Christ Jesus (Rom. 8:1 NIV). None. You are God's child and are promised full inheritance into His Kingdom.

If we fill our heart with the love of Christ, then our behavior will reflect that love. Wherever your heart is, that's where your treasure lies. Keep your eyes upon Jesus and focus on your faith, and you will begin to live out Jesus' new commandment, "Love one another as I have loved you" (John 13:34).

Paul summarizes this approach in the first two verses of Romans 12 (NIV):

> Therefore, I urge you, brothers, in view of God's mercy, to offer your bodies as living sacrifices, holy and pleasing to God—this is your spiritual act of worship. Don't copy the behavior and customs of this world, but let God transform you into a new person by changing the way you think. Then you will learn to know God's will for you, which is good and pleasing and perfect.

When we surrender our will to God, He can use all of us for His glory. You will be blessed in all that you do and have that peace of mind that passes all understanding. Trust in Him completely with all your heart and do not depend upon your worldly understanding—in all that you do be riveted on Him and He will direct your path (Prov. 3:5–6).

Let's face it. God is a loving Father Who wants to bless you beyond your wildest dreams. His plan for you is far greater than anything you can conceive (He's a bit wiser than we are). Rest in the knowledge that Father knows best. Just let go and let God. Give it up for the Lord, and you will receive His blessings both in this life and in the world to come.

11. The News
Emmett Holley

"It's cancer and you're going to do *what?*"

Let me start this story by telling you that I am no one of any significance in this world. I am just your ordinary guy with an everyday existence, which means that I work a lot and don't get to play a lot. I was raised in a Christian home with two parents, Bill and Nell who were better than I deserved. I got married and have a beautiful wife, Ellen, and two wonderful children Jessica and Will. With all that said, I consider myself to be greatly successful. On a scale of one to ten, my faith in God had only been stress-tested to around a two because everything had gone pretty well in my life. I guess I thought that I didn't need much faith.

On a warm Sunday afternoon in October 2006 around 4:45 p.m., I received a phone call that would rock my world. I had just had surgery on my left eye to remove a "routine cyst" or tumor. It had bothered me for a few months, and finally my wife had hounded me into finding out what was going on. The eye doctor had determined that the cyst/tumor was behind my left eye and needed to be removed. He had referred me to an eye surgeon who had agreed with the original diagnosis. The surgeon, Dr. Vorno had reassured me that these types of tumors were almost never cancerous. I honestly didn't expect there to be any problems.

I woke up from a surgery that seemed to last only a few minutes to find Ellen and Dr. Vorno standing beside my bed. My wife said that Dr. Vorno had some concerns. He said that the tumor looked suspicious. Even after being heavily sedated for a couple of hours, I could sense that the word *suspicious* was not a good thing. Later, I found out that Dr. Vorno had only cut the area open and closed it right back up after taking some tissue samples. I would be home for the next couple of days to recuperate with a patch over my left eye. Of course, there were some crazy thoughts going through my mind as to what was going on, but I figured that I wouldn't hear anything at least until Monday. After all, my surgery was on a Friday morning and I assumed that the doctors would be home for the weekend.

When the phone rang on Sunday afternoon, I saw on the Caller ID that it was the hospital, and I immediately answered. Much to my surprise, the voice on the other end belonged to Dr. Vorno who had performed the surgery—and he didn't sound as if he had just won the lottery. In a slow, broken voice, he said that the tumor was cancerous, and due to the type of cancer it was, in all likelihood, they would need to remove everything around the eye socket—including my eye.

"It's cancer and you're going to do *what*?" I asked. As tears started down my face and the words began to sink in, my heart sank to the lowest point in my life. I shook with fear and a chill ran up my spine like I have never felt before. Despite the fact that all kinds of people had conquered cancer and lived to tell their stories, in my mind, cancer was a death sentence, the end of life as I knew it. I hung up the phone and ran into my Ellen's arms. She already knew from my expression what the news was.

Dear God, please help me understand what is going on here? Confusion, frustration, fear, and a hundred other feelings rushed through my body. *I am just forty-four years old,* I thought. *I want to see my son and daughter graduate from high school, get married, and have kids. I have so many things that I need to take care of---I don't even have a will. What about growing old with my wife and working on my never-ending honey-do list?*

Needless to say, I was seriously overwhelmed with a severe panic attack. I can only imagine what was going through the minds of my wife and children. As a Christian, I knew in my heart that if I died, I would be going to Heaven (or at least cleaning up around outside the gates or something). However, I had not planned for this to happen in the next couple of months. I had not even considered yet what it would be like to have just one eye.

Since becoming a Christian, I learned that letting go and letting God control my life was the best decision that I could ever make. I realized through several "God Rescues" in my life that I wasn't the one driving my life's taxi—God was. I had made Him stop in a few places along the way where He didn't want to stop, but He had always been there waiting for me to get back in the cab after I screwed everything up. He has always been willing to take me back to His house to fix me back up and get me back on the road again. He has also sent some angels into my life as well. One angel who is a dear sweet woman that goes to church with my mother, gave me a scripture that I have never forgotten: I like the version that comes from the new Bible, *The Message,* most. The scripture is Proverbs 3:5–6:

> "Trust God from the bottom of your heart; don't try to figure out everything on your own. Listen for God's voice in everything you do, everywhere you go; He's the One Who will keep you on track"

It's pretty neat that God allowed me to remember this particular verse of scripture given the circumstances. Most of the time it takes me five minutes to find my wallet and truck keys in the morning and then leave only to discover that my fresh cup of coffee that I had prepared was left sitting on the kitchen countertop.

I knew that given this situation I would definitely have to have some help figuring out what was going on. For this task, God sent me another angel. Her name is Lynne. She and her husband had been what you might call our spiritual best friends for a great part of our life. Lynne came over and listened, cried, and even laughed with me for a while, but more than anything she helped me to understand what I had to do next. She told me that I had to "give this situation to God." Of course in the past, I would give everything to God with ten fingers attached to it so that hopefully "God" would make everything turn out the way I wanted it to. This time was different. I knew that I wasn't even capable of keeping ten fingers attached to it, and my walnut-sized brain couldn't even begin to grasp what was going on. The following is the prayer I prayed:

> *Father, I don't know why, but I am praising You for this situation. I know that You love me, but I am very confused and need Your help with this. Please help me, Ellen, Jessica, and Will as we go through this together with You.*

After I had finished praying, I sat quietly for a while waiting to see if God would reveal the wonderful answer that I needed. I have never heard God speak to me in an audible voice. If God *were* to speak to me in an audible voice, I would more than likely drop dead and meet Him face-to-face right then. However, God spoke to my heart, and said, "Emmett, I do love you, and I am going to take care of you. Believe it or not, I love your wife and children more than you do." I can't explain how God put this in my heart, but He did.

Very quickly, I was back for the surgery to have my eye removed and—we hoped--all of the cancer along with it. Over the next several months, I would go through thirty-two radiation treatments. My oncologist, Dr. Finch wanted to kill any possible cancer cells in that area of my head because of the proximity to my brain. My wife claims it fried the remaining two intelligent brain cells in my head.

During one of the countless visits back to the eye surgeon, Dr. Vorno had a slip of the tongue. He said, "We are going to leave the eye socket open for the next couple of years to observe it." At this point, I was a little confused by his comment and really thought the appointment was about how they would attempt a prosthetic eye. Then he said, "If you make it two years, we will figure out something then." The only word that I heard him say was *if.* That caused a sudden spike on the panic-meter. It was like the phone call that I had received at the beginning of my story. The phone was ringing again. *What now?* As I mentioned before, I had learned to let go and let God take control. He is driving, not me. God being the great Cabbie that He is, just turned around, smiled at me, and said, "Emmett, don't worry. Every day is a great day, whether I take you to your home or My home." That thought has comforted me to this day.

Well, it has been almost four years since my ordeal, and I must tell you how awesome God still is. I still have only one eye and really no hope for a prosthetic due to the extensive surgery, but God has allowed my heart to double in size. I now truly understand His saving grace, and feel His warm, loving embrace every day. He has shown me in countless ways how important each day is. I choose now to serve Him in a different way, and that is for Him to use me as His vessel. I am an imperfect vessel, but He still loves me and uses this worn, now-forty-eight-year-old vessel every day. I appreciate every moment of my cab ride, although I suspect that God might have kept me around so that He wouldn't have to do my honey-do list.

12. Sun Down

In the business world, bad news doesn't improve with age. In the medical field, an untreated wound will fester. In the restaurant business, dirty dishes will not wash themselves. As an owner and partner in a barbecue restaurant (now this is North Carolina-style barbecue, so we're talking *gourmet 'cue* here), I'm amazed at how fast dirty dishes can pile up.

It's funny, but that latter rule applies at home, too. As a bachelor, I have a significantly higher threshold and tolerance for dirty dishes than most, as I nonchalantly observe their sprawl across the kitchen counter. However, I will personally attest that there's a price to be paid for it. Have you ever left a cereal bowl with a few corn flakes left in it for several days in a sink? What could have easily been rinsed out with a quick squirt of water now takes an immense amount of effort of soaking, scrubbing, and sometimes scraping with a knife or other sharp object. Gorilla Glue doesn't hold as strong as a six-day cured, dried piece of cereal on the side of a bowl. What could have been solved quickly in the beginning now takes considerable effort after a completely avoidable, sloth-induced delay.

This "parable of the stubborn cornflake" especially applies to relationships in conflict.

When we get into a conflict with another person, the immediate reaction for the majority of us is to go the other way or leave it alone.

Most of us are conflict avoiders. There are some who enjoy conflict and initiate it, but that approach is like trying to douse a flame with gasoline. However, the path of least resistance is to let things go, hope they simmer down, and, like those dirty dishes, hope that they somehow miraculously get washed.

That's not a wise approach. Yes, if we become so angry that we've lost control of our emotions, we must first regain our composure. But as soon as we do, we must begin the reconciliation process. The longer we wait, the more that emotional wound will fester and the harder that "cornflake of distrust" will become attached.

In Ephesians, Paul–another bachelor, incidentally—addresses the importance of this sort of spiritual housekeeping: "Don't sin by letting anger control you. Don't let the sun go down while you are still angry, for anger gives a foothold to the devil" (Eph. 4:26-27 NLT).

There you go. The last thing we need to exacerbate a relationship problem is to allow the devil to assist in the counseling. He's always willing to give advice. It may be "pointed," but it's never cleansing. He thrives on conflict and he'll try to harden your heart like a two-week cured cornflake.

Yes, resolving conflict is challenging, and it is often more difficult with people that we really care about. The more we care, the more intense the emotion, and the more investment we have in jeopardy. But we have got to do it and do it quick. How important is this? *Very*. It is so important, look how Jesus described it.

> "Therefore if you are presenting your offering at the altar, and there remember that your brother has something against you, leave your offering there before the altar and go; first be reconciled to your brother, and then come and present your offering" (Matt. 5:23–24 NIV).

Our brother in this example might be our blood sibling or it could mean anyone. Now think carefully about this for a moment. This is Jesus talking about us giving our gift to God the Father Almighty. God, the Creator of the whole universe, Who deserves all glory, all honor and first priority in everything, wants us to delay our offering to Him and *first* be reconciled with the one with whom we have a disagreement.

Wow! If it's that important to Him, then it should be that important to us. God, fully wise and omniscient knows that the longer you wait, the worse it will get. This is not a suggestion (God never suggests)—it's a command. "Go and reconcile with the one with whom you have a disagreement. Then make your offering to Me."

Some situations may not be resolved in one night, and we can't control the actions of the other party, but we need to make sure before the day is done that our "brother" knows that we have left the door of reconciliation propped wide open. We have initiated our part, and we must continue to speak the truth in love until the dispute is resolved. Like those unwashed dishes, it may be a dirty business, but the sooner we get started, the sooner the stubborn cornflake is removed and the sooner life will start cooking again in the cleaned kitchen of our relationship.

13. Gone in 30 Seconds

Jack Wehmiller

I somehow knew that the six o'clock news was not telling us the whole story. From everything I had heard through emails and correspondence with fellow missionaries and a Pastor friend of mine, the Haitian earthquake of January 12, 2010, was affecting a lot more than the capital city of Port-au-Prince. On the island of Hispaniola, where survival for many was a moment-to-moment struggle on the best of days, there had to be a lot more going on than we were hearing about.

What was I supposed to do with these feelings? How was I supposed to help? One thing became clear: I felt compelled to leave my very comfortable place in Gainesville, Georgia. I had to go down there and see for myself. Retirement had given me the time and the resources to get involved and the call to help was too great for me to resist.

In the sixth chapter of the book of Isaiah, the Lord says to Isaiah, "Whom shall I send and who will go for us?" Isaiah responds, "Here I am, send me." That scripture became very real to me after the earthquake struck. Others were going to help provide relief, and yet while medical teams were leaving for Haiti every day, I was not hearing any reports of people going to Hispaniola's other nation, the Dominican Republic (D.R.), just over the mountains from Haiti. Pastor Pedro Johnson, a wonderful man living in the D.R. in the city of Barahona, told me that their hospitals were overflowing with Haitians. Knowing Pastor Pedro as well as I did and knowing that he was not prone to exaggeration, the situation sounded dire.

"Here I am, send me," became "Here I go" with supplies, prayers, and hope that I can make a difference. Little did I know of the heroes that I would meet on this trip. Little did I know of the life-changing experience I was about to have.

I landed in the Dominican capital of Santo Domingo and was picked up by a missionary from Puerto Rico. We went directly to one of the public hospitals in the city known as *The Cantreras*. I saw room after room and hallway after hallway filled with badly hurt Haitian men, women, and children. One area had eleven women on gurneys waiting for surgery. Remarkably, all of these people had somehow survived the ten hour-plus journey across the horrid pot-hole-laced roads from Haiti to Santo Domingo—but still they had to wait. The hospital staff told me through an interpreter that they would get to all of them, "in the next couple of days." I thought to myself, *Some of them won't make it two more days. Some will die in a foreign hospital hundreds of miles from their homes, and away from any of their surviving family and friends.*

My suspicions were confirmed about what was going on outside the immediate area of the quake. Next I pressed on to Barahona, just across the border from Haiti. Two more hospitals there had the same problems.

At the Sanchez Hospital, Pastor Pedro and I were confronted with an entire wing of the hospital dedicated to Haitian people hurt on that fateful day. We were in a hospital, so I could only imagine what it was like in the villages. Not only was the hospital overwhelmed with the tremendous number of quake victims with amputated limbs and broken bones, but it was painfully obvious that there was little if any fresh water available for these folks. I knew there was a scripture that spoke of giving a cup of cool water in the name of Christ, and this was what needed to be done. For two days we did just that. Young and old alike got water, juice, and words of encouragement. They got comfort from the group of nurses who were there with me. These women were from all over South Georgia, and they too had come to do what they could to help. These were humble, loving women giving of both their time and resources when both were greatly needed. The more I watched these heroes remove stitches, replace bandages, and give general care, the more I understood Jesus' admonition, "When you do it unto the least of these, you are doing unto Me."

I came to know several of the people to whom we ministered. I learned their names, ages, and what they were doing when the earthquake hit. I found out about friends and family who had perished or were missing and in doing so was moved to an entirely new level of understanding God's grace. In the midst of all that had happened, many of these men and women had not lost sight of who they were in Christ. The immediate lesson for me was never to try to reduce God to something that I could understand. I was to simply accept the grace in my life just as these souls had done. Displaced as they were, injured as they were, and in many cases having nothing more than the clothes on their backs, I saw a most wonderful sight: their Bibles at their bedsides. Someone had taken a mission trip to their town and shared the Gospel. Someone had lived out the Great Commission. Someone had come to this part of the world with "living water." I was passing out small material blessings to a physically battered group of God's children. In return, I was receiving incredible spiritual blessings.

On one very special day, I had decided to bring an interpreter with me to make sure that I was able to communicate with those that I would meet. Little did I know what that decision would mean in my life. I met a young woman named Miguelina Site. She had gone to the market January 12, just as she always did. Thirty seconds later, her injuries were so severe that her left arm above the elbow and her right leg above the knee had to be amputated. I gave her water and a smile. She gave me much more in return. Through Patrick, my interpreter, who was moving from room to room with me, I was told that Miguelina sang beautifully. I asked if she felt well enough to sing. She smiled, nodded yes, lifted her right hand in the air, and began to sing.

I have obviously not been to Heaven yet, but I now know what the music will be like. The entire song was in Creole, except the last three words. In broken English, Miguelina sang out, "Hallelujah, Hallelujah, Hallelujah." She looked at me again before closing her eyes to rest. I sat on the edge of her hospital bed, touched her lightly on the shoulder, and took in the enormity of that moment in my life. She understood the saving grace of Christ. It had become such a part of her that it was now sustaining her at an incredibly difficult time.

I went to minister and instead, my Haitian brothers and sisters ministered to me. I went to encourage and instead was encouraged. I took a simple cool drink of water and in return received a torrent of blessings. God was at work that morning in the Sanchez Hospital, Barahona, D.R. I learned a wonderful lesson from one of God's angels here on earth, and I will never be the same again. I understand much better than ever before the difference between a mountain and a molehill. My personal mountains appear much lower now and many of my molehills have ceased to exist. I went in hopes of being a small blessing to others. I came home incredibly blessed. I will go back to this part of the world many times---of that I am sure.

14. Déjà Vu

Basic Instincts

from sandbox
to schoolyard,
from playground
to paycheck –

they mix and they molt
and then march through
the Ages –

another generation enters
the arena, armed with weapons
of the Era –

clawing and gnashing, kicking and thrashing –
tongues a-lolling, chariots rolling –
truly nothing new
under the sun

Rick Saltzer

How often have you heard the maxim that history repeats itself?

How often have you heard the maxim that history repeats itself?

It often does, and in many cases that's not a good thing. During my extended season of prodigal son adventures, my sister made a needlepoint sign for me that still hangs on my wall today: "Experience enables you to recognize a mistake when you make it again."

Although America voted with emotion in 2008 (and perhaps not with enough wisdom) for Hope and Change (which can be good motives), the outcome unfortunately has been more of the same. Although some have gotten a thrill up their leg, the more fiscally sane have gotten a chill down their spine. Small bailouts have become large bailouts. Stimulus packages and major legislation pass through Congress so fast that they're not even read. Deficit spending has skyrocketed, and this grotesque spending is the most appalling. Our country has trillion-dollar deficits forecasted annually for most of the next decade—that's a trillion dollars each year of spending more money than what is taken in.

How much is a trillion dollars? A trillion one-dollar bills laid end to end would not just go to the moon and back, it would go past the sun. Using the shopaholic spending rate scale, if you had spent $10 every second since the birth of Christ, you would still have enough change left over to be wealthier than the richest twenty Americans *combined.* Want it framed as an annual rate? We're spending nearly $32,000 per second more than we make—our nation just lost $100,000 while you read this sentence.

To call this spending money like a drunken sailor would be—to quote Ronald Reagan—an insult to drunken sailors. This is not financial mismanagement. This is insanity. If our government continues to spend at its current deficit pace, the U.S. debt will soon be somewhere past the dwarf planet Pluto, which is beyond insanity. As Ben Franklin warned, "When the people find they can vote themselves money, that will herald the end of the republic."

The real irony is that these forecasted deficits assume that the rest of the budget is accurate. This is a budget that plans to pay for all this additional spending through streamlining existing costs and reducing waste. Name any government program in our country's history that has accomplished such a feat. The United States Postal Service forecasts a $7 billion shortfall in 2010 and government-run Amtrak has never made a profit. Fannie Mae and Freddie Mac went bankrupt, and ask any car dealer how "streamlined" the "Cash for Clunkers" program worked.

The government is simply not structured for cost efficiency. It's like riding a mule in the Kentucky Derby. It lumbers along like an aircraft carrier where scheduling stops and turns require miles of ocean to plan and carry out. It can't turn quickly, and if it could, expensive aircraft would slide off the flight deck. It is powerful and offers strength and protection, but it is not designed for maneuverability. A big, controlling government is not a problem solver, but a problem creator. It's not intentional; it's just how it functions. It takes discipline and moral turpitude on the part of our elected officials of both parties to maintain its integrity and to keep its growth under control, for the more it controls, the less freedom we citizens have.

Our country faces serious challenges, and our fiscal woes are a symptom or manifestation of a deeper cause. Our moral compass is out of alignment. Capitalism and wealth creation are not bad things. Profit to a business is like oxygen to a human—go without it and death ensues.

Money is neither good nor bad; it is how we use it that matters. When control over the people's freedom and wealth redistribution becomes the focus, when lust for power becomes the motive; when the ends begin to justify immoral means, then we get into trouble. When self-preservation and party line take priority over our nation's needs, we definitely have a problem. We have one-percent of our population in jail right now. That's a sad testimony to our nation's moral condition. We owe incredible sums of money to other countries, and we are being outperformed economically by China, a Communist nation—that's absolutely embarrassing!

We do need change. However, the change we need must come from within. To truly implement effective and efficient policy, we need a change of heart. It's time to clean up our act and get our priorities straight. Experience should not only tell us when we are revisiting mistakes of our past. It should provide us insight as to which way we should go.

We need to turn back to the source of our power and our greatness. We are not great because we are cool and smart people (although that helps). We are not great because we have abundant natural resources (although we do). We are great because we are a nation under God and we acknowledge Him and His Son in how we conduct ourselves in our way of living. We as a nation have strayed away from that concept, and we desperately need to return to it. We have a loving and patient Heavenly Father, Who, like the father in the prodigal son parable, longs for our return.

This is the key to saving our country. I encourage all of us this year, whenever possible, to contemplate 2 Chronicles 7:14 and to go to the Lord in prayer: "Then if My people who are called by My name will humble themselves and pray and seek My face and turn from their wicked ways, I will hear from Heaven and will forgive their sins and restore their land" (ESV). God spoke this incredible universe into existence. He can easily solve our financial, healthcare, military, and employment woes if we humbly call upon Him in prayer.

Pray daily for our nation. Pray before this next election that we the people may have the discernment to elect godly leaders. Pray for our leaders that they may seek the Lord and His wisdom. If we as a nation go to the Lord in prayer, imagine 300 million voices petitioning the LORD, "If we confess our sins, He is faithful and righteous to forgive us our sins and to cleanse us from all unrighteousness" (1 John 1:9 NASB). He will heal our land, restore our prosperity, and protect us from evil. He is the Way and the Truth and the Life, and there is none greater. He has vowed to forgive and restore us, and His performance history is 100 percent in fulfilling what He promises.

15. Child's Play

My dad was born in 1924, five years before the stock market crash and the start of the Great Depression. At the time of his birth his father was fifty-two and his mother was forty-two. Like many in rural North Carolina at that time, you didn't worry about getting to the hospital in time as he was conveniently born right there in the home. He was the last of nine kids, and naturally, being the baby of the family, he was the smartest and best looking.

Dad had many of the stereotypical "growing up on the farm" stories—like walking two miles to school, barefoot, in the snow, uphill, both ways—but many of them were actually true. He did feed the chickens and milk the cows before school. The icebox was truly a box under the house with a big block of ice in it. His mom cooked over an open flame stove—not gas but wood-burning—and the house wasn't heated by a heat pump, but by multiple fireplaces, and all the wood needed to cook and heat the home wasn't cut by a chainsaw, but with an axe and a two-man crosscut saw.

Dad marveled that he probably had witnessed the greatest change in technology in human history as he went from plowing fields behind a horse (or in some cases a mule) to watching a man land on the moon.

Having served in the U.S. Navy, my favorite story that Dad told me about his childhood was his excursion as an underwater diver.

My dad's best friend growing up was his cousin Tom for whom I am named. Tom was a P-38 Lightning pilot in World War II and was killed in action during the Invasion of Normandy in June 1944. If you saw the movie, *Saving Private Ryan*, well, he's probably in that same cemetery where Tom Hanks's character was buried. In fact he was killed the same day—June 16, 1944.

While they were growing up together, Tom and Dad were well known locally and more commonly referred to as Frank and Jesse, as in Frank and Jesse James. They pulled their fair share of pranks.

One time while in an adventurous and inventive mood, Tom and my dad decided to try out underwater diving at the local pond down on the farm. The tools needed were an air source (bicycle pump), a long air hose, and a diving helmet. For the diving helmet, Dad "liberated" a large pot from his mom's kitchen. (When you come from a family of nine, there are lots of large pots around.) They cut a hole in the bottom of the pot and inserted a bicycle tire valve in the hole. This valve was connected to the long hose, which was connected to the bicycle pump. The concept was that one would wear the big pot over his head, go into the water, and just walk around on the bottom of the pond while the other would pump in air from the bicycle pump. Considering that the pot was metal, I don't know what they planned on "seeing" while walking on the bottom of the pond. (After listening to this story, I was really glad that Dad went into pharmacology and not engineering.) Now Tom was two years older than Dad, so when it came to who was selected for the "dangerous missions," Dad somehow was always chosen to be the test pilot, test diver, or whatever fancy title they used for the role, which in reality translated to "white rat."

When the day of the "big dive" arrived, Tom and Dad gathered on the little pier that jutted out a few yards from the edge of the pond. In order to make sure that Dad would sink to the bottom once he jumped into the water, they tied bricks to the bottom of his shoes.

So now "Frank and Jesse" were ready for their first venture into underwater diving. Not even Norman Rockwell could picture this. Two young boys in overalls, standing out on a rickety little wooden pier, one manning a bicycle pump and the other with bricks tied to his shoes and a big metal pot on his head. (Alas, my dad was now a pothead.) Dad slowly shuffled out with his brick-laden shoes to the end of the pier. Tom was manning the bicycle pump, ready to start pumping as soon as Dad jumped in the water. I imagine there was a long, pregnant pause once Dad reached the end of the pier. Yet with complete faith in his cohort, Dad jumped in.

I suppose that seeing a kid jump into a lake wearing a pair of old coveralls with bricks strapped to the bottom of his shoes and a big pot on his head might be quite amusing. It seems that was the case, as Tom didn't pump any air at all, but rolled on the pier laughing. The bricks did their job well, and Dad plunged rapidly to the bottom. The bottom of the pond was very soft mud, and the bricks sank in pretty deep.

So now Dad was at the bottom of the pond, his feet tied to bricks that were stuck in the mud; he has a big pot on his head, and no air. When his feet wouldn't move, Dad got a little scared. He had to reach down, untie his shoelaces, and slip out of his shoes to swim up to surface and breathe.

That night I think Dad got two whippings—one for cutting a hole in his mom's pot and the other for losing his shoes. Hearing stories like this made our family amazed that he made it to old age.

The other truly amazing part of this story is the trust that Dad had in Tom. It almost was a fatal trust. Call it naïve or foolish, but despite the dangerous circumstances, my dad had so much faith in his cousin that he literally trusted him with his life.

We should obviously avoid putting so much faith in another person, but this innocent trust is what we should place in Christ. As Jesus said, "I tell you the truth, anyone who doesn't receive the Kingdom of God like a child will never enter it" (Luke 18:17 NLT). What is so important about receiving God and His Kingdom like a child? I think there is an innocence of trust in our early years. A child's natural inclination is to trust first, and this trust is pure and genuine. There's no figuring out the angles, questioning of motives, or deciphering of agendas. Once that trust has been broken or damaged, the heart becomes a little more hardened—a little more wary and less trusting.

As we get older, this innocent trust is tempered with doubt and suspicion. We even develop some countermeasures such as shrewdness, cunning, and perhaps even a few of our own methods of deception and white lie spin. It's difficult to openly trust again when we've been hurt or burned, so in response we've spent years building our own defenses. We've all been betrayed in a relationship or perhaps a business deal. It's painful so we set up protective measures. In many cases, we take these protective measures into our relationship with God. What's the point of building a fort if you're going to exist outside the walls? How can we put our full trust in God and just open ourselves up with complete vulnerability?

One defensive approach many of us take is that when we pray we "bargain" with God—engage in quid pro quo arrangements such as, "I'll do this or give up this, Lord, if You'll do this for me." Ever done that? Then we sometimes use that to justify excluding God from our decision-making if a situation didn't go how we wanted. We rationalize: *I asked God for help in this area of my life (based on my terms and conditions) and He didn't come through for me so I'm now going to handle this on my own.* It doesn't work that way or it certainly will not work out well that way. God *can* be fully trusted. He made us and loves us beyond our comprehension and yes, He also *knows* and *desires* what is best for us. We are to trust Him with our whole heart and lean or depend not on our own understanding (Prov. 3:5). It is that childlike faith, that trusting and humble heart that pleases

God. "Therefore, whoever humbles himself like this child is the greatest in the Kingdom of Heaven" Jesus told his disciples (Matt. 18:4 NIV).

Proverbs 3:6 goes on to say, "In all your ways acknowledge Him. And He will make your paths straight." The word "acknowledge" is a little weak in today's culture. It truly means to be focused on Him, or—as another translation puts it—"to seek His will in all that you do." He will make our paths straight or our path clear in our mind on where we are to go.

What a great promise. If we follow it, have a humble heart, and trust completely in the Lord, not only will we be considered "great" in the Kingdom of Heaven, but figuratively, God will keep us out of deep water and free us if we get stuck in the mud.

16. A Grandmother's Love

Doug Hanson

During a fall visit to an orphanage in Dornesti, Romania, in 2000, I had been asked by fellow missionary, Ruben Popet to join him on a short ride in a station wagon to the Dornesti train station on the other side of the Suceava River to meet one of the orphans' grandmothers. She was coming by train to visit her granddaughter Nicoleta for the day, and the mile-long walk would be too much for her, especially since she often would bring gifts for Nicoleta and the children.

She had already arrived when we got to the train station. She was dressed in typical Romanian garb with a black skirt, a number of layered blouses, a sweater, and a dark brown scarf. The weather had cooled by late September, and she was ready for a sudden cold blast from northern Ukraine. Dornesti is only five miles from the Russian border.

With Nicoleta's grandmother were two large plaid bags loaded with fresh apples. No doubt, she had handpicked these from random trees across the area just before the trip. During the fall, it is most common to see families and individuals carrying long sticks to knock down free apples from the many trees that dot the landscape. How she was able to tote these heavy bags onto and off of the train was a miracle in itself. Both Ruben and I grabbed a bag, headed for the station wagon, and loaded her up for the short trip to the orphanage.

As we backed up into the orphanage's food-service dock, all the children came running. They seemed to have a sixth sense of when guests would be coming, particularly if the guests had gifts. We lifted the bags onto the dock and poured the hundreds of apples onto the concrete floor. The kids each got to have one, and the rest were sorted for pies, jams, and jellies. There was great laughter and appreciation for her thoughtfulness. Nicoleta was among the greeters, and her beautiful dark, Gypsy skin and black hair set off her smile like a picture. She was very glad to see someone from her immediate family.

Romanians consider children to be orphans if only one of their parents is missing or deceased. During the Communist years, most of the children were abandoned at birth, or several months afterwards, when their parents either determined that they could not feed them or when their patience with a hungry, crying child had vanished. Nicoleta was one of those children, and her grandmother was not able to care for her though she still had the love and presence to keep the relationship intact.

During the late morning, Nicoleta and her grandmother chatted and walked the orphanage grounds. They both had a lot of catching up to do. They enjoyed lunch together in the pine-paneled dining room, most probably soup, bread, and porridge. Her grandmother would stay through the early afternoon.

Meanwhile, after lunch, I had moved outside for some afternoon photographs. During the day, nomadic shepherds would come through the Suceava River banks with their huge flocks and patiently move with their dogs as their flock fed on the lush grass. Shepherds would stay with their flocks around the clock, seven days a week. In their native dress and with their crooks, they were quite a photo op.

It was while photographing one such shepherd that I glanced up behind the soccer field and noticed Nicoleta's grandmother walking along the railroad tracks on her way to the train station for her return trip home. She had traded apples for rolls of carpet and was laboriously carrying the two bags filled to overflowing with pieces of wool carpet. She was bent under the weight, and for a person of her age, she was making a super-human effort to keep moving.

I tucked my camera inside my jacket, zipped it over the lens for protection, and began to run around the perimeter of the soccer field to the train tracks. I knew the route to the tracks and across the Suceava River; it was the route we took every morning with the kids to their school. It was a good run to the tracks, about two U.S. city blocks. Once I arrived at the tracks, the route grew more level, but it was still difficult because of the discarded ballast and old concrete ties from the Communist era. I couldn't see Nicoleta's grandmother as I reached the edge of the bridge. Supposing that she was farther ahead of me and over the crest of the bridge, I ran faster, only to see a black object crumpled at the other end of the bridge, lying in the rail bed. Her carpetbags were strewn out with rolls everywhere. She was not moving.

My heart began to pound as I approached her. She was moaning and obviously injured. I heard the rumbling of a CRT switch engine as it appeared around a curve and rapidly approached us on the same track. I had to do something.

As an American visitor to the orphanage, the children enjoyed teaching me a few Romanian words. Fortunately for me, one of them was the word for *stop*: *opreste,* pronounced "o-presh-te." I stood in the rail bed in front of Nicoleta's grandmother, waving my arms frantically and shouting "Opreste! Opreste!"

I got the attention of the engineer, who brought the huge engine to a squeaky stop near her body. He was expressionless. He had nothing to say. His demeanor seemed to say, "Why are you doing this? You're wasting my time." I thanked him for stopping with another word I had learned from the kids—*multemesc*—and lifted the woman to her feet. Both of her knees were bleeding from the sudden contact with the sharp ballast, but I could tell that she was a strong woman and wanted to move on. She had a train to catch at the Dornesti station.

Sliding the carpet rolls back into the bags, I hoisted them up onto my shoulders, grabbed her black purse, and gave her my right arm to hold as we began our slow walk to the train station not yet visible ahead. How was I to know how injured she was? She could not tell me a word. She grimaced as she made her way along the side of the tracks. I knew we were getting closer to the station, as more tracks converged while we walked.

As we approached the station after a forty-minute walk, we could see a passenger train sitting on the tracks with the engine idling. I needed to get the grandmother to a place of rest, so I spotted one of the wooden benches, like a church pew, common to old train stations. She slumped into the seat exhausted.

A train conductor quickly approached her and asked her what her destination was. "Suceava?" he asked. Suceava is a large city 30 miles to the east near the Moldovan border, and the train must have been scheduled for there.

"Da," she said.

He asked her, "Billet?"

She fumbled through her purse and found her return ticket, handing it to the conductor.

He pointed to the ticket and then to her. "Your train," he said.

We walked to the nearest entry door for the coach in Class 2—the cheapest seats possible. There, the carriage's blue door was open, and the enormous steps awaited her to board. As she approached the first step, I could readily see that her injuries were too much to allow for an easy climb. There was no help from the conductor standing nearby, so I gently placed my two hands under her bottom and with one motion, pushed and lifted her onto the platform. I grabbed the two bags and placed them on the platform beside her.

The conductor blew a shrill whistle, one long blast. The train began to move and pull out of the station. The grandmother looked at me, patted her heart twice, and blew me a kiss as she rolled away. I was emotionally spent and broke down in tears.

In fact, I cried all the way back to the orphanage as I walked along the train tracks and across the bridge. I was so amazed at how God would use me, a visitor who did not know the language in this small village halfway around the world, to assist this loving grandmother who wanted to make a difference in her granddaughter's life and home. At the same time, He would stop not one but two trains in the process to show His grace to us both.

17. Real Climate Change

So how's this global warming working out for ya? As I get ready for another snowfall here in Atlanta, I am thankful for global warming or else things would be a lot worse. God only knows how much snow could now be falling here, and my fellow Atlantans do not fare well on the roads in snow. Of course, I know one year does not a climate change make, but now that the manipulated scientific data is exposed and the real data is starting to come out, it seems the earth has been on a ten-year cooling trend. That should ease the minds of many a polar bear.

The shameful part is that there were so many involved in the false science of it all. Science has but one mission—the relentless pursuit of the truth. Over time the scientific community has developed sound practices in pursuing the truth. It's called the scientific method. However, the scientific process used to study climate change in many cases was inverted or at least dyslexic. Instead of stating a hypothesis, gathering, and analyzing the data, and then deriving a conclusion, they stated a conclusion, and then manipulated the data to support the hypothesis.

Perhaps these scientists will next ask Al Gore, our former vice president, Nobel Laureate and Academy Award-winner, who produced the movie, *An Inconvenient Truth*, to create a dyslexic titled sequel that's more appropriate to their methods: The Truth is Inconvenient. Unfortunately, even the former Vice President needs to brush up a bit on his numbers. In an interview in November 2009 with Conan O'Brien on NBC's *The Tonight Show* (before Jay Leno took it back), Mr. Gore stated that the interior of the earth is extremely hot, several millions of degrees.

Hold the presses. Well, there's your trouble. We've found the source of global warming. The earth is about 8,000 miles in diameter and thus it's only 4,000 miles to the center. If the center of the earth is several millions of degrees, then using even the most conservative heat transfer equations, the surface of the earth would be several thousand degrees. We would all be like President George Bush 41's speech of becoming little points of light. Yep, we'd all be little points of blurred light, for we would all be running around on fire like the human torch from Fantastic Four. The world would be a planet full of screaming alphas fires. (Scientific note: a burning human being would be considered an alpha class fire and most likely they would be screaming—thus a screaming alpha.)

The center of the earth may be several thousands of degrees, perhaps even as high as 20,000 degrees Fahrenheit, but that's a far cry from several million.

Okay, so the former vice president's math was a little off by a factor of a hundred or so. Does that mean his whole message is wrong? Certainly not, but it does bring to light that an emphasis on the truth supported by multiple scientific studies must be diligently maintained, and a calmer, more rational approach using reason over ranting needs to be employed. There is no doubt that spewing megatons of pollution into the air has an adverse effect on our planet. The magnitude of that effect is truly unknown. The science of climatology is very complex. It is obvious that we need to create a comprehensive plan for our country as well as be a leader for the world to migrate toward more eco-friendly forms of energy, but we need to do so in a well thought out manner.

We have been appointed by God to serve as stewards over this planet, and we need to preserve and protect the environment and the creatures that live in it, including ourselves, as best we can. Genesis explains:

> For God said, "Let us make human beings in Our image, to be like Us. They will reign over the fish in the sea, the birds in the sky, the livestock, all the wild animals on the earth, and the small animals that scurry along the ground." Then God blessed them and said, "Be fruitful and multiply. Fill the earth and govern it. Reign over the fish in the sea, the birds in the sky, and all the animals that scurry along the ground"(Gen. 1:26, 28 NLT).

The first step the United States should make is to significantly reduce our dependence on foreign oil. This is a national security issue. Though this solution appears to be moving backwards as it means that America should initiate more drilling here in the United States, it will buy our country time and keep our money "in house" to help finance and develop a bolder transition plan to greener energy such as natural gas and nuclear power. Solar, wind, geothermal, tidal, and biomass (using animal waste to create fuel) energy programs all sound great, and they are...they're just not feasible on a large scale for the immediate future. Producing more domestic oil creates taxable revenues (we can't tax foreign countries' oil profits) that can fund incentives programs to fast-track the development of these alternative fuels into viable forms of energy for mass use.

The current plan in Congress, "Cap and Trade," aims to significantly raise taxes on carbon-based fuels, thus making them more costly and alternative fuels more competitive. Even the president admitted that energy costs will "skyrocket." That may not be a wise approach in our current queasy economy. Families who are barely making it will not be able to heat or cool their homes, and the effect on the elderly living on fixed incomes will be devastating. Every business in America will be adversely affected as energy costs are built into every product and service that we buy and sell. Using a healthcare analogy, a patient needs to be reasonably healthy before a major surgery in order to survive it. Our country is currently not healthy enough to undergo such a major "energy change" surgery. The patient may die on the operating table as our economy would in all likelihood crash.

Finally, this effort must be global in scope. All nations must do their fair share. If one nation enacts stringent pollution and energy controls while other nations do not, it will have about the same effect of a man walking into a smoking room and choosing not to smoke in order to improve the room's air quality. The only reward he would get for such an effort is a cough. Consensus and cooperation must be committed before costly controls are put in place.

Now that you've weathered some more hot air (perhaps an undocumented source of global warming) on this subject, there's a far more dangerous warming problem that faces the world. This warming lasts forever. For many, it is an inconvenient truth. A whole genre of movies goes along with this as well. I'll pick one as an example: *Night of the Living Dead.*

If you were a zombie, and there was a way to bring zombies back to life, would you want someone to tell you? Or, better yet, to try to help save you? Well, there are a lot of walking zombies out in the world—going through life, doing their thing, thinking they are alive, yet dead in their sins. Most are oblivious to their plight. They lack the truth.

Jesus tells a story in Luke 16 (verses 19–31) about a rich man and a poor beggar named Lazarus. Many people consider this another one of Jesus' parables, but I doubt it, for Jesus never used names in His parables. This is a real story of a poor beggar and a rich zombie. In Jesus' telling of the story, the rich man lives lavishly, dresses in purple and fine linen, and enjoys all the finer things in life. The poor beggar named Lazarus lives near the rich man's gate and longs to just eat the scraps from the rich man's table. Even dogs come by to lick his sores.

Both men die. Now Lazarus is carried off by angels to Heaven and brought to comfort with Abraham—the patriarch of the nation of Israel. Meanwhile, the rich man suddenly realizes that though his life was good on earth, all the while, he had been a zombie. Now he was in Hell.

The rich man cries out to Abraham, "Father Abraham, have pity on me, and send Lazarus to dip the tip of his finger in water and cool my tongue, because I am in agony in this fire." (This is the never-ending, personalized global warming.) The conversation continues. Abraham replies:

> Son, remember that in your lifetime, you received your good things, while Lazarus received bad things. But now he is comforted here, and you are in agony. And besides all this, between us and you a great chasm has been fixed, so that those who want to go from here to you cannot, nor can anyone cross over from there to us.

The rich man replies, "Then I beg you, father, send Lazarus to my father's house, for I have five brothers. Let him warn them, so that they will not also come to this place of torment."

Abraham replies, "They have Moses and the Prophets; let them listen to them."

"'No, father Abraham," the rich man says, "but if someone from the dead goes to them, they will repent."

Abraham says to him, "If they do not listen to Moses and the Prophets, they will not be convinced even if someone rises from the dead" (Luke 16:24–31).

It seems some zombies are not all that bright. Even seeing someone who rises from the dead will not convince them to depart from their walk of death. Well, that's where we are today. We have Someone Who has risen from the dead, and His name is Jesus. All those who place their hope and trust in Him will get to hang out with Abraham and those in the paradise of Heaven. That's the wise way to live. Those who live like zombies, oblivious to the saving grace of our Lord Jesus Christ, will go on to experience the very ultimate in global warming.

We all should do our part in minimizing waste and avoid increasing pollution to preserve our planet's natural resources. We should not pass on an ecological mess to future generations for them to clean up. More importantly, we should not leave a spiritual mess for future generations either. Physical garbage is bad, but spiritual garbage is far worse. Get cleaned up and focus upon this one truth: *Jesus Christ is Lord, and trusting your life to Him is the only way to live.*

Are you on fire for the Lord or cool to the whole subject? Be careful. Your temperature may change dramatically in the next life. When it comes to this world, the only way to truly save the planet is to introduce everyone to Jesus Christ. Trusting in Him is the first and most important step to solving our problems. Now that's something worthwhile that we all can warm up to.

18. The Dash

One of the most powerful tools in the business world is the effective use of project management. Standard operating procedures adequately handle the business while in steady state. However, any initiative, expansion or improvement objective is best achieved through the use of "Best Practice" project management techniques.

The first step in defining a project is to define your goals by creating an accurate mission statement. Then you develop a "To Be" or Future State. Then next step, (which should be a given), is to describe your "As Is" or Current State. Then you design and build the best road map or migration path to go from where you are (Current State) to where you want to be (Future State).

Properly defining your Future State is critical. Without an accurately described future or end state, you never know when you get there or, even worse, you don't know if you're going in the right direction. You wouldn't get in your car and then have someone ask you where you are going, only to reply, "I don't know" (unless you're having one of those "senior moments").

Our lives here on earth are not that complicated. We all have the same end state. At some point we will give that bucket one final kick, the music will stop, the lights will go out, and the party will be over.

My first job was working for the city of the mighty metropolis of Graham, North Carolina, mowing graveyards and digging graves. Though it was a dead business, I dug it. Besides, everyone was dying to go there. Mowing cemeteries was a great leadership opportunity as on my first day, I already had a lot of people under me. None of them would listen, though. I guess that's why they eventually let me go as I just couldn't cut it. (Alright. I'm done. I was just having too much pun.)

During my "mowings," it was interesting to see the different types of tombstones. There were old ones and new ones, big, elegant ones, and small, simple ones. Many had quotes and elaborate sayings, others were just plain, but they all had one thing in common. Besides the name, they had the date of their birth and the date of their death with a little dash in between.

In that little dash was their entire life. It contained all their efforts, hopes, and dreams whether they were realized or not. The sum total of their earthly life—all they ever did was contained in that one insignificant symbol.

That seems a bit understated doesn't it? As we go through life in the ironic dichotomy of simultaneously living and dying, we know that the hairs on our head are numbered. For some men that's not too many. As the sappy soap opera saying states, "Like sands through the hour glass, so are the days of our lives." So how's the sand passing for you? Is your life a beach or more like 50-grit sandpaper? How are you doing your dash?

If we convert our life into a project plan, then we need to have a well defined Future State. Life is a journey best traveled with a destination in mind. Knowing where you are going and the best way to get there is the optimum method for doing your dash and doing it well. Along the way, we should go Army and be all that we can be.

But wait there's more. No, it's not a free bamboo steamer or a ginsu knife. It's great news. This is especially true if so far, your dash isn't doing so hot. When the lights go out on your earthly life, it ain't over.

There's another dash! This dash starts at the date of your death, and it goes on forever. This is the real Future State.

This Future State is the one we must get right. It's your final dash. The proportions are correct as well. Our first dash is but a blip—the second is a line to infinity. You can screw up your first dash beyond all human comprehension, yet in a heartfelt instant get realigned and ensure your second dash is completely right. This is not the recommended strategy of course, but that's incredible hope. As long as you are alive, there is no Current State too terrible that cannot be corrected. Accepting Christ as Lord of your life guarantees you the right Future State.

The author of the book of Hebrews stated it very succinctly, "And inasmuch as it is appointed for men to die once and after this comes judgment" (Heb. 9:27 NASB). Someday we all will have to give an account of how we lived—how we did our dash. If somewhere along the way in our first dash, we accepted Jesus Christ as our Lord and Savior, then our second dash is cash and it's going to be a bash. No matter how good or bad the first dash went, this one will be awesome beyond words. You will certainly dig it. If you do not put your trust in Christ, then your dash is trash and well, that's not a place you should be dying to go.

Don't wait until your last hairs. That's not just hairy; that's scary. It's truly grave danger. Do the dash right by doing it with Christ. Then you will be in line for a great reward. For on that final Day of Judgment, our Lord will ascribe these words to your dash in life, "Well done, good and faithful servant."

19. The Confusion That Confused Me

Rick Saltzer

The image of a Christmas tree on the front page of that morning's *USA TODAY* yanked my attention from the maddening scent of the coffee counter to the colorful headlines of the newsstand. I instinctively wondered what politically correct Christmas news could possibly dominate above-the-fold space in "The Nation's Newspaper." Perhaps, it was a nicely timed fluff piece designed to distract reader attention from the high unemployment and economic woes. Alas, in a moment of caffeine-deprived weakness, I allowed my curiosity to overwhelm my sensibility, and I shamefacedly purchased a media product. I then quickly shuffled out of the store with my head down, bitterly chiding myself for consciously donating a buck to the liberal press.

I settled into the comforts of my front seat to wearily peruse what I expected to be the usual condescending, secular diatribe on the trivialities of "the winter holiday season." Surprisingly, the story actually had nothing to do with Christmas per se; however, it did provide some valuable, albeit alarming, insights into the composition of America's contemporary church via a recently concluded Pew research survey. To me, the real kick in the head was the inexplicable new perspective that groups of "Christians" and their leaders have begun to take on Christianity. Some of the key findings of the study detailed in the article were:

- Roughly two-thirds of U.S. adults, including many professed Protestants and Catholics, have begun to adopt elements of Eastern faiths and New Age thinking.
- Adherence to one clear faith is diminishing, and mixing/matching beliefs and practices is now becoming the new norm of worship. One researcher opined that the findings indicated a heightened degree of spiritual and religious openness, rather than a lack of seriousness.
- A majority of Americans have changed their religion one or more times, with most citing unmet spiritual needs or a change in their religious or moral beliefs.
- Some 92 percent believe in "God"; however, 70 percent maintained that different faiths can lead to eternal life and also felt that there were several ways to interpret the teachings of their religion.

The data seemed to indicate one clear conclusion on the status of faith in America: "rampant confusion"–the phrase used by one particular Christian leader quoted in the article to describe the revelations of the Pew research.

Ugh! Satan, the father of doubt and confusion, had apparently done his work well. Most adults probably would have agreed that the spiritual and moral Christian underpinnings of this nation have been eroding for a while, but the size of these numbers was scary. Suddenly, my twisting stomach and contorting brain convinced me to dump out the rest of my coffee and remove my tongue from my cheek while I fretted over that singular phrase: "rampant confusion."

As I sat there brandishing a coffee-stained newspaper for an hour or so, two quotes that dealt with the concept of confusion kept banging together in my head. Ironically, Ayn Rand, a well-known atheist, had written, "The hardest thing to explain is the glaringly evident which everybody had decided not to see"—sort of a one-line equivalent of

The Emperor's New Clothes. Secondly, John MacArthur, the prominent Christian pastor and leader, had observed that the single biggest problem facing Christianity was "the terrible decline in Bible literacy."

The confluence of these two thoughts kept dragging me to the same conclusion: The confusion in Christianity depicted in the research and the subsequent article was either caused by not knowing the Truth (ignorance), or, worse yet, knowing the Truth but lacking the fortitude to accept or declare it. I confess I found myself confused by all the confusion.

For those confused Christians, a thorough reading of John's gospel should answer every question. Jesus Christ repeatedly and clearly stated His identity and His purpose. He clearly and repeatedly stated that He was the only way to eternal life, and explained how believers were to behave in their earthly lives. He clearly and repeatedly explained the eternal consequences of not accepting Him as Lord and Savior. He did not provide any other options, alternatives, or Plan Bs for us to contemplate. What was so confusing about that? Consider:

How many ways are there to eternal life? See John 14:6.

Must a Christian be born again? See John 3:3, 7.

What is eternal destiny of believers/unbelievers? See John 3:15–21, 6:40, 8:24.

Who is our "father" if we have not accepted Christ (i.e., other "religions")? See John 8:37–47.

Did Christ bring a new religion, a new belief-system, some new ideas, or the Truth? See John 1:17, 4:24, 8:31–32, 14:6, 18:37.

Again I asked myself, what could have been so confusing about these passages to a Bible reader? Or was it that *confusion* was, in fact, being confused with *rejection*? Was the Truth truly obvious in the Bible, and people didn't recognize or understand it (MacArthur's assessment)? Or was it more accurate to say that the Truth was plainly revealed, but not acknowledged and accepted, as in The Emperor's New Clothes—

something that, as Rand put it, was glaringly evident, but willingly overlooked?

After two hours of noodling over all these questions and attempting to sort through all the confusion, I was left with a basic answer that seemed to resolve the issues raised by the data above: Jesus Christ is Truth, and personal acceptance of and belief in the Truth results in eternal life for the believer. Any beliefs, faiths, religions, and so on, that are not of the Truth (John 8:37–47, 14:6) are untrue and, therefore, false. Believers in that which is false will be eternally condemned. These are God's rules, not mine, and they are plainly written. God's rules are not politically correct. We won't have any rights, and we won't get a phone call or a lawyer. There'll be no protests, demonstrations, or boycotts. Follow the rules and we spend eternity in Heaven—reject them and spend eternity in Hell.

I was finally shaken out of my trance by the sound of my jingling cell phone. I let it ring while I reflected on the unexpected turn my morning had taken, all because I had broken my own vow not to subsidize the left-leaning media. I chalked it up to another example of the price one pays for lapses in self-discipline, although a part of me suspected that this was one of the most productive mornings I had ever experienced.

Now it was time for that coffee.

20. Who's on First?

Our family has a wonderful tradition. Despite being scattered across four states, we all pick a weekend in December where we return to our original homestead and celebrate Christmas together. Each year we have a friendly family feud in a football game between the kids and the adults, go see a movie together, and in an all-hands-on-deck effort, work together to prepare the Christmas Eve meal (which stresses Mom a bit, having so many in the kitchen). It's always an enjoyable time, and yes, we do it because we want to, but it happens because we make it a priority.

A recent family tradition (if you can call it that) was initiated by my older brother in that he was the first one in the family lineage to make Eagle Scout. He led the way, and I, being the younger brother, followed suit. Now, all four of my nephews have achieved the rank of Eagle Scout, and my niece received her Gold Award, which is the highest rank in the Girl Scouts.

I cannot compliment enough the benefits of Scouting and the principles it teaches in building strong character traits as boys transition to young men and girls transition to young ladies. A critical component is having good leaders, and I personally was blessed with having two that were outstanding. The twelve points of the Scout Law are timeless in their application. A Scout is Trustworthy, Loyal, Helpful, Friendly, Courteous, Kind, Obedient, Cheerful, Thrifty, Brave, Clean, and Reverent.

These are as valuable today as they were when the Boy Scouts started in 1910. If you don't have a satisfactory set of character traits that you want to establish, then these are a great baseline.

Building character is like building a building. You need a firm foundation, and ensuring that this base is laid correctly is paramount. When constructing a building, there is one block or stone that is more important than all the others are—the cornerstone. It is the first stone placed when building a foundation, and all other stones are laid based on the position of the cornerstone.

If you're more of the interior decorator type, then use wallpaper as the analogy. When putting up wallpaper (a great project for young couples wanting to test the strength of their marriage), the first piece is the most important because each piece placed after it is positioned based on the alignment of the first piece. If the first piece is laid incorrectly, then by the time you get around the room, you'll have a geometric mess. Then you may hear, "Uh, honey, why don't we just paint the room?"

In value setting and character building, there also exists a cornerstone. Of all your priorities, principles and values, there is one that is the most important, the value that supersedes all the rest. Everyone has a cornerstone. What is yours? What's the most important thing in your life? What should it be?

If you don't know what the most important thing in your life is, you need to pause for a moment and figure it out. This is your calibration point. This should be front and center in your brain and within your heart. The value to you of everything else in this world is based on what you have as your cornerstone. If you choose the wrong cornerstone or your cornerstone is improperly placed, then your whole building is out of alignment. If you don't get that fixed, then your building won't pass code, will be condemned, and will be torn down. That's not a good thing.

In the Gospel of Matthew, Jesus told a parable about a landowner and his vineyard (Matt. 21:33–41) that described the coming ruin of the

Jewish nation because they rejected His teachings and explained how the Gentiles would be blessed for receiving Christ. In verses 42–43 Matthew writes:

> Then Jesus asked them, "Didn't you ever read this in the Scriptures? The stone that the builders rejected has now become the cornerstone. This is the LORD's doing, and it is wonderful to see. I tell you, the Kingdom of God will be taken away from you and given to a nation that will produce the proper fruit." (NLT).

The United States, who incorporated Jesus as "Our Lord" in its Constitution, has been an incredibly fruitful branch on the vine of Jesus. We declared that God (not our own government) has given mankind certain inalienable rights of life, liberty, and the pursuit of happiness. Freedom is our nation's most cherished gift. The greatest freedom is freedom from sin, which can only be obtained through faith in Jesus Christ. As our country's leaders direct us away from this precept, we have already begun to notice that our productivity has started to decline, and our stature in the world has diminished.

If you don't have Christ as your cornerstone, your building is misaligned. In the end, you won't pass code. Like a house built on sand, your building will not survive when the rain and winds come, but will fall in a great crash (Matt. 7:27). Jesus calls such a builder "foolish." However, if we have Christ as our cornerstone and hear His words and put them into practice, we are "like a wise man who built his house on the rock. The rain came down, the streams rose, and the winds blew and beat against that house; yet it did not fall, because it had its foundation on the rock" (Matt. 7:24–25 NIV).

We must start first with Christ. He is the Rock on which we stand. With Christ as our cornerstone, we have a building of character that can withstand any storm. Then for daily living, "Seek first His kingdom and

His righteousness, and all these things [that you need] will be given to you as well" (Matt. 6:33).

There are many important things in our lives. We have our bills to pay, family to support, relationships to maintain, work to do, food to buy, healthcare needs, and all the events big and small that fight for our attention. God knows our needs. He promises that He will provide for us. If we have Christ as our cornerstone, if we make Him a priority, and we daily seek first His kingdom in all that we do, then all that we need will be added or provided unto us.

It's a great promise. In these stressful times, it offers both hope and peace of mind. There's a simple saying: "No Christ. No peace. Know Christ. Know peace."

21. My Destiny

Perhaps the most powerful gift ever bestowed upon humanity was the gift of choice. Our capacity for self-determination or the opportunity to choose our autonomous destiny through conscious decisions despite our personal limitations presents us with a vast array of near-endless possibilities. This gift from our Heavenly Father is not His greatest gift. His greatest gift is the gift of His Son and the redeeming power of salvation offered through acceptance of Jesus Christ as Lord and Savior. "For God so loved the world, that He gave His only begotten Son, that whoever believes in Him shall not perish, but have eternal life" (John 3:16 NASB). This gift of redemption enables the believer to share a future eternal life with our Heavenly Father. However, note the awesome power in terms of consequences in God's gift of choice. The gift of salvation is not forced upon us; it is not a guarantee or a right. Thus, the greatest of all of God's gifts to mankind cannot be received without the human choice of accepting it. But do we have a choice? In a universe with an all powerful and all knowing God Who knows what we will ask and do before our asking or doing, are we exercising a legitimate act of choice, or are we simply behaving in a predicted manner that was predestined before the foundation of the universe itself—mere actors upon the stage of life reciting our lines until the play comes to its final conclusion?

It is obviously difficult, (in fact, it is impossible) for finite Man to truly grasp the infinite—for the natural to comprehend the supernatural. An omniscient God knows all that can be known. His knowledge is infinite. However, infinity can take on many forms. In mathematics, we can sum consecutive numbers to infinity and have the result of infinity. We can likewise only add all the odd numbers up to infinity and we still get infinity. We can leave out the number 19 and add the rest or leave out prime numbers or some other variant, so pardon the pun, but there are an infinite number of ways to reach infinity. Are there varying degrees of omniscience as there are varying degrees of infinity? If so, does that violate the concept of an omniscient God?

As humans, we seek knowledge and understanding, but are limited in our capacity to absorb its full meaning. This limited capacity of knowledge is expressed in Paul's first letter to the church in Corinth: "For now, we see in a mirror dimly" (1 Cor. 13:12). In light of our limitations, does this apply to our perception of choice or the true reality of our ability to choose? Does our ignorance of the complete truth fool us into believing that we are making decisions, creating and being the original source of our own thoughts and then acting upon them, or are we merely reacting and behaving in response to an extremely complex set of environmental factors both internally and externally—a predictable pattern easily discerned by an omniscient God?

Theoretically, it makes sense that an all knowing God knows everything. That is the definition of omniscience. He is a God so powerful that He merely spoke the universe into existence. A God Who is eternal and unchanging and Who created time and space and stands outside of His own creation. As the Creator of time, He stands outside of time and can view past, present, and future simultaneously. Everything that exists is under His domain, and there is not even a rogue molecule operating independently outside of His control. Such a universe would imply that the concept of randomness does not exist with God.

The universe, despite its great breath and complexity, is fully known throughout time and space, and there are zero degrees of freedom from which it can deviate. Some would propose that this is not to say that no other possibilities exist, but an omniscient God knows both all the plausible outcomes as well as the real outcomes. This definition of God's omniscience is maximized; however, there are profound consequences of such an interpretation.

Technically, the argument rests on the question that if something is foreknown, is it determined? The seemingly logical answer is that if an outcome is precisely known, then it is truly determined. Thus, when we see a fair die being rolled where the probabilities of rolling numbers one through a six result are equal, we consider each number to be equally probable. If it is foreknown that a three will appear, then the probability of a "3" is 1.0 or 100 percent, and the probability of the other numbers is zero. If something has a probability of zero, does it exist? If so, then everything exists, and that leads to nonsense.

Addressing a situation at the more complex human decision-making level, suppose we have a person, P, at time t, in environment E (where E accurately describes every attribute of P's internal and external surroundings, temperature, humidity, luminescence, gravity, intellect, emotions, etc., down to the very cells, molecules, and free radical electrons cruising around in E and the body of P), and P faces, for simplicity's sake, the four choices of A, B, C, and D. If God has designed the universe such that He foreknows that the person, P, in environment E at time t will always choose D, then the probability of D is 100 percent and the other so-called plausible options in fact do not even exist. What we perceive as choice in our ignorance is actually a predestined result.

That seems somewhat boring.

We have a loving Heavenly Father Who desires us to have a personal relationship with Him, not only in this world, but also in the world to come. He loves us so much that He sacrificed His Own Son on our behalf to reconcile and redeem us from our sin so that we may have an eternal relationship with Him. Peter tells us that God desires that no person should perish, but that all should have eternal life (2 Pet. 3:9). God is actively involved in our lives and has been throughout human history. There are many references throughout the Bible of divine visions and dreams, angel visitations, burning bushes, and pillars of fire, to name just a few. The most demonstrative display was the visitation upon earth of Jesus Christ, God Incarnate, Who came for our salvation, but also to show us in human form what God is like. When Philip asked Jesus, "Show us the Father," Jesus responded, perhaps exasperated, "Have I been so long with you and yet you have not come to know Me, Philip? He who has seen Me has seen the Father" (John 16:8–9 NASB).

We now can potentially see within our finite minds the impending conflict of the infinite love, infinite knowledge, and infinite power of God. Why would Peter state that God desires that no one should perish, when God already knows, before even initiating creation, that many will? Does that now become a limitation on God's infinite power? Have we sacrificed God's omnipotence to maximize God's omniscience? Granted, God is the Potter and we are the clay, and God can make us into whatever He chooses, whether it be a beautiful vase or an ugly spittoon. He can choose to save some and ignore others. It's not about us; it's about Him. Yet how many people over the course of human history will be saved? If salvation is a desire of God, what percentage of humans will make it? Is it 80 percent, 50 percent, or perhaps below 20 percent? For a God who loves His creation, Who allowed His Son to be brutally tortured and killed for our behalf, is this the best He can do?

Ah, but we have a choice. The gift of salvation is a gift that can only be accepted by our choosing to do so. Is this really a legitimate free act of choice, though? If our decision is completely known before we even decide, then this is not a choice but a result. Life is as described in the behaviorist model. You have stimuli and then a response. The Pavlov model: A bell rings and a dog slobbers. We, in ignorance, think we are choosing, but in fact we are reacting to an environment of external factors and internal electronic impulses, and chemical reactions. Dendrites fire, chemicals are released, and actions are engaged based on the exact nature of the surrounding external and internal environment. No cognitive value-added or spirit induced "thought" process takes place—it simply becomes a physics problem (granted a very complex one) of a given set of circumstances that will produce a known result.

Jesus said, "Behold, I stand at the door and knock; if anyone hears My voice and opens the door, I will come in to him, and will dine with him and he with Me" (Rev. 3:20 NASB). What is the purpose of His knocking if He already knows whether or not we will answer? Is it some academic exercise? Is it something to be used during the time of judgment, where Jesus tells those unfortunate ones who did not answer, that "Hey, I knocked." Could their response be, "But you knew beforehand I wouldn't hear you. Why didn't you knock louder?"

In Jesus' famous Sermon on the Mount, He encourages us to ask, seek, and knock, and it is in the present participle context of ask (and keep asking). He further gives an example, "Or what man is there among you, when his son shall ask him for a loaf, will give him a stone? Or if he shall ask for a fish, he will not give him a snake will he? If you then being evil, know how to give good gifts to your children, how much more shall your Father Who is in Heaven give what is good to those who ask Him." (Matt. 7:9–11 NASB). If we being evil (meaning being sinful) can give good gifts to our children, then how much more so will our Heavenly Father give to us?

For all parents and prospective parents, consider this scenario. If you wanted to have a child and were making preparations to have a child, and God said to you, "You can have this child, but his or her name will not be in the Book of Life. The child you will have, at the conclusion of their earthly life, will be destined to live eternally away from Me and in eternal Hell and damnation." Would you have that child? Would you bring a life to this earth knowing that upon conclusion of that child's earthly life, they would live a life of eternal torture and absence from God? I do not think so. A parent's love or in this case a prospective parent's love for their future child would be too great to do such a thing. So if God's love for us is far greater than anything we can imagine, then how can He knowingly allow such things to happen? Why would He go through with a creation that He foreknows will produce so much eternal pain and suffering? Granted, He is God and we are not. He is capable of such an act, but it goes against the very nature of the love, mercy, and grace of God.

Maybe we do in fact have a choice—a legitimate act of our own free will that is originally sourced from the spirit that dwells within our human bodies. Its capability may be an infinitesimal piece of the whole universe, barely measurable, barely distinct, but indeed ours. It is that infinitesimal piece that allows a sliver of a degree of freedom to give us the legitimate ability to choose and the responsibility of that choice. Yet, how can this occur outside the awareness of an omniscient God?

In medieval times, Biblical scholars pondered such questions as, "Can God create a rock that He cannot lift?" It's amusing yet a little silly, and often atheists try to use such a question to invalidate the omnipotence of God. In the end it is foolish as it is like asking if God can create a square circle. No such thing exists nor can it by its own definition. However, in trying to resolve the tension between God's omniscience and man's free will, we're asking a somewhat different question that appears well within God's capability without absurd conflict: Can God create a random number? In order for it to be random, there can be no logical basis for its outcome and it cannot be known before it is created.

Perhaps science has given us a hint about this. In both chaos (the butterfly effect) and complexity theory, there are certain mechanisms and events that despite precise replication cannot be consistently modeled to predict a certain outcome. In quantum physics, we have the Heisenberg uncertainty principle, which states that we cannot know with certainty both a particle's position and momentum (or where it is and where it is going) simultaneously. Perhaps these are "measurement" problems in that science has not learned enough to be able to solve these dilemmas, but it could be evidence of design that God built this subatomic imprecision into the very fabric of our universe.

As John Polkinhorne, the physicist-turned-theologian describes, the universe operates more like a cloud than a clock. In fact, it is not even randomness, but instead of pure exactness and perfect precision (the clock model), the universe operates across a range of probabilities (the cloud model). If matter behaves this way, then we as humans (made up of matter) can have slight deviations in behavior and thus possess the actual ability to exercise choice. In this model, our person, P, in environment E, at time t, has legitimate choices of A, B, C, and D, where D is equal to some number slightly less than one and the remaining choices have associated probabilities that when all totaled add up to one or 100 percent.

Though the difference is mathematically minute, the effect is astronomical; for this conceptual view of man's free choice makes the universe an exciting and dynamic place under the dominion of a loving Heavenly Father. When God created the universe, He did so from a choice of many possible worlds to create. When He formulated the natural laws to govern the universe and created mankind in His own image, then this vast number of possible worlds was reduced to a smaller number of feasible worlds. If He designed man such that He retained absolute and complete foreknowledge of every single event and outcome, then these feasible worlds would reduce to one actual world.[1] Though from our limited viewpoint and knowledge, this world is still very dynamic, from God's perspective, it is a static preordained set of events that occur as planned. The future is mathematically a straight line, and thus the rejoicing in Heaven over the conversion of a doomed sinner to salvation is a planned event. Such a concept conjures up the image of angels in Heaven reading God's Plan of the Day and remarking, "Oh, I see at 7:18

HST (Heaven Standard Time) that we're to give a shout that Joe Smith has received Christ as his Savior." This concept unfortunately precludes the existence of hope in Heaven or anywhere else for that matter. If Joe Smith's name never appears on those preprinted celebration pages for converted sinners, then there's no chance and no hope for Joe.

The Bible states that when God created the universe, He said, "Let Us make man in Our image, according to Our likeness; and let them rule over the fish of the sea and over the birds of the sky and over the cattle and over all the earth, and over every creeping thing that creeps on earth" (Gen 1:26 NASB).

I am not sure who the "Us" is in this verse, the Father, Holy Spirit, and Son pre-incarnate, or if it was some type of Creation Committee formed in Heaven. But something magical may have happened in that creation. In man, He gave a spirit that is eternal. That is understood, but maybe in that creation He gave us something else. God is the ultimate Creator. Nothing existed prior to His creation, and everything that does exist is due to His creation. By designing a universe with subatomic imprecision (quantum indeterminacy) and by making mankind in His own image, out of His great love for us, He gave us a sliver of His sovereignty through the legitimate ability to freely choose to truly exercise our own free will. He is the great Creator, and we being created in His image share a piece of that ability to create—the ability to create a thought and choose to act upon it. This ability, in conjunction with the continuous active involvement of God in the world and in our lives, enables us to participate in God's plan whether we choose full obedience, partial obedience, or disobedience to His will. It is an active, dynamic world where God is working all around to accomplish His will while allowing us the freedom to choose. Pictorially speaking, the future in this model looks more like a tree branch. All the branches are still fully known by God, but our collective choices through God's gift of free will help determine which "branch" mankind follows.

Such a gift is incredible and powerful. It does not place us outside the domain of God or outside His authority, nor does it enable us to thwart God's overall plan. The degree of latitude and freedom is still way too small as God in His infinite wisdom has already foreseen all possible outcomes. The multiplicative effect of error or imprecision (errors compounded upon errors) has already been forecast and is contained within God's overall providential will. It does give us, however, this infinitesimal sliver of autonomy, a power of true, legitimate choice—an ability to choose that possesses enormous consequences. Just observe the history of man. If Adam and Eve had not succumbed to temptation, we'd all be hanging out having fun in the Garden of Eden. Contrast that to the time of Noah where God had to intervene and basically reboot the system of mankind. Those are perhaps the divine guardrails that God has put in place. It is through this incredible, sacrificing love that God gave this gift to us and He desires that we would take this gift of choice and use it wisely. Unfortunately many will not.

The wise choice for each of us is inherently obvious. Give back to God what He has given us—to submit our legitimate ability to freely choose and forego our self-centered will to His will for us and let the power of the Holy Spirit work through us to accomplish His will. Our finite minds cannot improve upon the plans of an infinite God. His love for us is beyond human comprehension, and our trusting fully in Him with our choices is the wisest thing we can do. Our Master and role model, Jesus Christ, when facing the pending horrible execution of crucifixion prayed three times to the Father "to let this cup pass from Me," but concluded by saying, "Yet not as My will, but as Thy wilt" (Matt. 26:39). Like our Lord and Savior, we must make our own conclusions on what to believe, what to do, and who to follow—the most important decision we will ever make, but indeed through this powerful gift from God, our legitimate and free will opportunity to choose.

22. Name Calling

> "What's in a name? That which we call a rose by any other name would smell as sweet."
>
> —William Shakespeare, *Romeo and Juliet*

So how important is a name? Is the Bard of Avon also the Bard and Brains of Branding? For new companies, branding is considered a very important enterprise as the brand is the initial image the consumer sees—the opening statement about your company. If a rose was actually called a pukglobenstinke, it may smell as sweet, but perhaps few would dare try to take a whiff of it.

According to *Business Week* in 2009, the value of just the name, Coca-Cola, is worth over $68 billion. That's a lot of soda. Other top company brand names are IBM, Microsoft, Nokia, McDonald's, and Google. Proverbs states, "A good name is more desirable than great wealth. Respect is better than silver or gold" (Prov. 22:1 GWT). From this analysis, it seems a good name is great wealth.

So is the value of their company caused by their name? Or has the value and quality of what they do and the goods and services they provide caused their name to have value?

Although a catchy jingle, name, logo, or slogan can enhance a company's overall marketing, the major metric for the value of a name is based on the quality of how the company performs. If its smell is desirably sweet, even a pukglobenstinke will develop a loyal sniffing fan base. It is who the company is, what it represents, what it does, and how well it does it that makes a good name.

When Enron became an infamous name, Arthur Andersen, a multi-billion dollar "Big Five" consulting firm was handling much of Enron's accounting practices and books. Arthur Andersen firm started in the early 1900s and developed a reputation for honesty and a zeal for maintaining high standards within the accounting industry. For many years, their motto was, "Think straight, talk straight."[1]

However, when faced with the conflict of following proper accounting practices and reporting procedures or trying to enhance their client's financial position, the Andersen firm chose unwisely. After the Enron scandal broke, the company went from think straight, talk straight to straight down the tubes. The end came quickly as most of the business was sold off to other accounting firms. Although the firm has never formerly closed or gone into bankruptcy, in a period of about eighteen months it went from over 100,000 employees worldwide to now around 200.[2]

Arthur Andersen lost its good name.

On the *O'Reilly Factor* on the Fox News Channel, host Bill O'Reilly bragged about the Fox cable channel being the most trusted name in news as 49 percent of Americans trusted Fox. This was way ahead of CNN and more than twice that of MSNBC. Fox should be proud of being the leader as they are the most "fair and balanced," but in general, it is still an honor among thieves. The sad fact is that over 50 percent of Americans don't trust Fox, and they trust the other networks even less. The mainstream media industry should be ashamed of their loss of integrity and trust from the American people. To quote Bernie Goldberg, the mainstream media has become the "lame-stream media," and the entire industry has lost its good name.

The current public opinion of our members in Congress is at an all-time low, and this rating has been down for several years. The American citizenry watch with disdain the appalling behavior of our politicians. We see their backroom deals, schmoozing with special interest groups. We see their motivation for self-preservation and priority for their party over the people of this country. They are public servants elected to provide a public service. Yet, they possess and project this arrogant attitude of "public serve us." Our elected leaders are losing their good name.

On the individual level, this can happen to us, too. Our name is all that we have in this world, and we should be very careful to protect it. Although there are lots of Peters, Pauls, and Johns in the world, not many parents name their kids Judas these days. Sometimes a stain lasts forever.

We should be wise in how we walk in this life and careful in what we do. We should protect our name and ensure that it is esteemed with honor, integrity, and righteousness. Jesus told His disciples, "Whoever wants to be the most important person must take the last place and be a servant to everyone else" (Mark 9:35 GWT). Never let greed surpass integrity. Never compromise or shortcut your values and principles to achieve an objective. Be kind and treat others with respect and honor. Perform the Golden Rule of do unto others what you would want them to do to you. Another proverb states, "Never let loyalty and kindness leave you. Tie them around your neck as a reminder. Write them deep within your heart. Then you will win favor and a good name in the sight of God and man" (Prov. 3:3–4 NLT).

These are not hard concepts to understand, but if you are not careful, they can be hard concepts to continuously follow. Sometimes it only takes one slip, and a great reputation can be forever tarnished. As the saying goes, it takes only one "Aw shucks" to wipe out ten "attaboys."

So don't shuck things up—protect your "brand name" and honor God with it.

23. Answering the Call

—Kathryn Mae Rogers

When I was eleven years old, I was saved at Sardis Baptist Church and baptized in Lake Lanier. To bring me to this milestone in life were Christian parents who taught me many things in life including many things about Jesus Christ.

Moving forward to the year 2002, I was looking at turning fifty years old in three years. My question to myself was, *what is it I want out of the rest of my life?*

I started to think and to pray. It is time to get back to me. I needed to start finding ways to fill my time because my son, Jonathan, would soon be driving and wouldn't need me as much. I wanted and continue to want to be the best parent possible and encourage his independence. I had a lot on my mind and I wasn't happy with the way my life was turning out.

The company I worked for wanted me to attend a Dale Carnegie course. I asked my friend, Steve, to start praying that someone else would be going so I could at least have someone I knew to hang out with. He told me he was going. That was a wonderful relief. He is such a nice person, which would make this fun.

During the time of attending the Dale Carnegie class, Steve and I found we could talk about anything. At this point Steve and I became very close friends. As the Dale Carnegie class came to a close, I started hearing about the Stephen Ministry, which trained laypeople to be listeners. Steve showed me the website; I started gathering information. The time came to sign up for the Stephen Ministry class. I was excited and afraid at the same time.

In January 2003 the Stephen Ministry classes began. I clung to every word being taught and could not wait for Thursday nights.

A prayer was said in class for two Stephen Leaders to step forward. My chest was pounding. *Me? Surely not me.* The next day I called a current Stephen Leader. I asked him if we could talk that day. I told him of my feelings and requested that he try to talk me out of this.

I told the Stephen Minister Leader, "Not me—I'm too shy."

The leader told me, "If God is calling, you had better answer." He said that the church would pay the expenses, and all I needed to do was give a week of my time.

I thought, *A week of my time…for me? Is this how I am going to find me again?*

Commissioning Sunday was approaching. Leaving for Leadership training was coming, and I would be leaving soon. This is not exactly what I had been looking as way to keep busy. But I knew God was calling, and I needed to answer.

I invited several friends to Commissioning Services, including Steve. I really wanted him to come; we had become very special friends. I also knew he was praying hard for me. He was supportive in many ways, including encouraging me to become a Stephen Leader. By the end of the Leader training and my return home, I knew I needed some changes in my life.

Steve and I had talked every day, and I knew he was praying for me. I had also realized that he was in love with me, and I with him. I asked myself, *Why am I in love with this wonderful man at this stage in life? So many things must happen for us to even think about anything beyond a friendship.* I had prayed for something to fill my time in the evenings, but being in love and the thoughts of marriage were not on my list.

I started praying again and started to try and make sense of all of this, often asking myself, *Why me?* We had learned in Stephen Ministry about how to accomplish our goals. We also learned how sometimes God's hand worked through other people, and how all things occurred in God's time.

Okay, I thought, *I am going to be a leader, so I need to put all these skills I have learned to the test.*

Process takes patience, and patience is not one of my strong points, but I was determined to give it a try. I prayed that I would know what to do and would know it was the right thing.

I gave God a laundry list of things that I felt needed to happen; selling two houses, buying a house, as well as many more things. *Okay, I am going to see. This process thing is supposed to work.*

Slowly things began to happen, and in time, everything I had asked for had happened. *Okay, this process thing does work.*

Steve began coming to First Baptist Church with me and soon felt the call to move his Church membership to First Baptist. Steve asked me to marry him after all of our individual goals were met. I was afraid of so many things. I started praying again. I felt secure enough in accepting his proposal after many hours of prayer. We announced our plans for marriage; the affirmation came from our friends, and so many blessings came that I knew God was in this. We started planning a wedding and a celebration. As plans were being made, I knew God had this plan for me and I was truly blessed.

The training and skills from Stephen Ministry was a contributor to my learning to listen to God and be obedient. God has blessed me with a partner who is beautiful inside and out.

I thought of Psalm 46:10: "Be still and know."

A little voice directed Steve and me to Kirkwood Baptist upon moving to St. Louis three years ago. The voice came from two of our precious friends at First Baptist Church, Gainesville, Georgia. Their words were, "If you must go, find Kirkwood Baptist Church." Their words kept repeating in my mind.

Kirkwood Baptist had been waiting for us as a church family, ready to receive us and love us; a church family to walk with us on our journey of life in St. Louis. Steve and I are blessed. The prayers of our church family have carried us many times in the past year. I thank them for that.

Soon after visiting Kirkwood and having a conversation with the pastor, I knew why we were in St. Louis. God was using Steve and me to bring Stephen Ministry to Kirkwood. It was an answer to Steve's prayer that I would find a way to use my Stephen Ministry Leader skills. God's unlimited amazing grace provided me with the time and energy to make a difference at Kirkwood, and I am humbled.

Kirkwood Baptist Church welcomed Steve and me and we are grateful. God led us here and we are blessed.

24. Truth or Consequences, Part I

It is interesting to note that many people have the misplaced concept that science and spiritual faith are at odds with each other. They consider that science is full of laws, experimental proofs, and mathematical equations that substantiate fact, whereas faith is a magical leap into the unknown with a hope and a prayer. Nothing could be further from the truth. In fact, that is exactly what they both seek—the truth. Science and faith (or religion, which represents the organized body of faith) are completely complementary and both are in search of the same objective. They both seek the truth, the whole truth, and nothing but the truth, for falsehoods in either are both dangerous and detrimental. No religious person wants to believe in something false any more than a scientist wants to promote an inaccurate theorem. The truth is the ultimate prize for both, but the approach is often different. Science tends to ask the question of how, whereas religion tends to ask the question of why.

A commonly used example is if I wanted to make a pot of tea and I put a kettle of water on the stove to boil. Later, another person enters the room and asks why is there water boiling on the stove. One answer is that the conductive heat transfer from the gas flame has increased the enthalpy of the water to surpass the phase change energy requirement to cause the water to convert to steam; and the other is that I wanted to make a pot of tea.

There does exist an ultimate truth. This is truth with a capital "T." It truly (pun intended) is the whole truth and nothing but the truth. It is Truth. No human knows this Truth; in fact, no one even comes close. There are far more unknowns than knowns. There are probably far more unknown unknowns (things we don't even know that we don't know) than what we know. Ignorance is bliss, you know (Yeah buddy, how 'bout them dawgs.). To know Truth requires omniscience. One must know everything about everything to know Truth. Now, just because we cannot know this Truth or even come close to the total knowledge required of omniscience, doesn't mean we should throw up our hands in surrender and seek bliss via ignorance (although it does seem that a few people have pursued this strategy).

As such, despite the absence of complete truth, many assertions can be made that help us understand why things are and how things work. In science, there is a path progression toward truth based on the level of knowledge obtained through the depth and breadth of experimental validation. Ideas start with a hypothesis, grow into a theory, and then become confirmed into law. We have laws of gravity, thermodynamics, electromagnetism, and others where repeated experimental validation and mathematical proofs confirm their status. Theories have less degree of certainty than laws, such as the theory of relativity, chaos theory, and evolutionary theory. These are classified as theories because substantial amounts of data obtained through experiment and mathematical models support the presumed conclusion, but there still remains some conjecture. A hypothesis is the infant form of a future theory where insufficient testing and analysis have yet to occur.

In religion, the approach to understanding why things are they way they are is analogous to the scientific approach but obviously not the same. They both use a sense of logic, but religion relies more on experience than experiment. To the hardcore scientist, that sounds a little flaky—karma does not fit well into a test tube. Yet experience is just as valid as experiment even though it does not occur in a laboratory. Without experience and interpretation, the world becomes a very boring place. From the scientific perspective, hearing Jimmy Page of Led Zeppelin stroking his guitar riffs on "Stairway to Heaven," Lynyrd Skynyrd jamming on "Freebird," or listening to Beethoven's Fifth Symphony simply become vibrations in air of multiple frequency and amplitude. A Rembrandt or Picasso is merely chemicals of varying pigments spattered upon a canvas. That's pretty dull. Combining experiment and experience together, however, they added richness and depth to understanding the truth and the existence of the real. The more tools we employ to view the world, the greater our understanding and perception of Truth.

This combined approach is not uncommon in the everyday functions of our society. Think of a criminal trial. You have the CSI guys performing the science aspect in their analysis of the scene, ballistics testing, and gathering samples of DNA, and you have the testimony of eye witnesses (experience) and the evaluation of motive (interpretation) of the suspect. It takes all of these characteristics to get a more accurate picture of the truth.

Belief, however, in and of itself may be perfectly aligned, partially aligned, or in complete opposition to the truth. It depends on what you believe. In the general trade of stocks, the person selling believes the stock will go down while the one buying believes it will go up. One of them has to be wrong. A common fallacy is the sense that the intensity and sincerity of one's belief enhances its truth. Unfortunately, there is no correlation between the two. Another falsehood is that because belief is personal, it's a blank check for whatever one wants to believe, and it is impossible or politically incorrect to state that one belief is superior to another. Most everyone has heard of the tooth fairy. If I were to believe in the tooth fairy with all my heart, it still wouldn't make the tooth fairy real. I could envision a grander role for my tooth fairy in that upon my death that she would escort me to the pearly (white) gates of Heaven where I would get my crown of gold. I could dream up wonderful things and believe in them with complete sincerity, but no amount of faith would make it true. Religious faith, like science, is only valid when it represents the truth. Truth is the universal measuring stick for everything.

Whether a scientist, a theologian, a blue collar faith-walker, or anyone else, we should all seek the truth and let truth establish our principles and guide our actions. Ignoring or denying the truth is never beneficial. We even have a name for that way of life as "living in denial." It's denial of what? It's the denial of truth, and those who live in denial will always struggle.

We each start out in this world with the common individual truth, "By the grace of God, I am what I am" (1 Cor. 15:10a). We are each unique, but all are born into sin, and none of us live our lives perfectly. The unfortunate truth is that the payout or wages of our sin is death. Thanks to God's immeasurable grace, the story doesn't end there:

"But the gift of God is eternal life through Christ Jesus" (Rom. 6:23).

"Truly, I tell all of you with certainty, the one who believes in Me has eternal life" (John 6:47 ISV).

When Jesus tells you to believe something with certainty, then accept that as an undeniable truth.

25. Truth or Consequences, Part II

Many people remember the comedian Flip Wilson and his famous saying, "The devil made me do it." Although the devil doesn't make anyone do anything, he certainly encourages misbehavior. Satan is a defeated foe, as Christ kicked his pointy tail at Calvary. His fate is sealed, and he is doomed to spend all eternity in the Lake of Fire. However, until that time comes, he is still a powerful adversary, and his whole purpose in life is to exalt himself and to thwart the purposes of God.

God is all-knowing, and therefore possesses total Truth. Satan is opposed to God and therefore is opposed to the Truth. He is the father of lies, and there is no truth in him (John 8:44). Since everything about him is a lie, he has nothing to offer but a marketing plan devoted to deception. Paul even warns us that Satan sometimes disguises himself as an angel of light (2 Cor. 11:14). Knowing that we do not have the whole truth ("for presently we see in a mirror dimly," 1 Cor. 13:12), he needs to bend the truth just enough to lead people astray. Unfortunately, he is very skilled at this.

The devil has made great progress over the last fifty years. Here in the U.S. (the largest Christian stronghold), his efforts have gotten prayer out of schools, made fornication and abortion mainstream, greatly increased the rates of divorce and unwed pregnancies, and moved homosexual behavior way out of the closet. Breaking down or perverting the family unit is a strategic goal as it promotes dysfunctional behavior into future generations.

Here are just two of his many recent marketing campaigns that, when combined, may fool multitudes. When you analyze it, you'll have to admit that it's a clever plan. In military terms, it combines a decoy frontal assault that may capture only a few of us, but which will, if successful, drive a majority of us towards what seems to be a safer alternative, but is really an ambush.

The direct frontal attack consists of the recent ad campaigns run by various atheist organizations. The devil considers atheists as useful idiots, people who—though they don't even believe in Satan's existence, are nonetheless important accomplices in his efforts to rule the world. Some of these ads ran during the Christmas holiday, stating that there is *no* "reason for the season" and that we should just be good for goodness's sake. In Europe, another effort launched the ad, "There's probably no God. Now stop worrying and enjoy your life."[1]

Let's contemplate the wisdom of this last slogan, for it is fraught with foolishness and deception. First, the first sentence paraphrases a Bible verse. Psalm 14:1b actually states, "There is no God." Of course, this is a perfect example of taking a line out of context as the whole verse is, "For the fool says in his heart, 'There is no God.' They are corrupt, their deeds are vile; there is no one who does good." If you want to be a fool (or a useful idiot for the devil), then don't believe in God.

Second, those who have accepted Jesus Christ aren't worried about their salvation. Only the unsaved should worry. If they sense it, then it is the Holy Spirit trying to trouble their consciences to turn them from their destiny of death. For there are none righteous, not even one—all have sinned, and the wages of sin is death (Rom. 3:10, 23, 6:23).

Notice also, that saying that there's "probably" no God is not as shocking as the blunt statement that there is no God. All Satan needs is a "You're probably right" response. Lulling a person into apathy about

God is just as big a success for the devil as turning someone to directly oppose God. One must proactively choose God. Not deciding or caring is the same as a "No" vote.

Finally, even the logic is faulty. If there was no eternal life, then at death, everybody loses equally. If there is an eternal life provided by God, then those who put their trust in Him win, while those who don't lose. So even using the ad's logic, if you bet on God, even with their suggested improbable odds, you still may win. If you don't, you'll *always* lose.

The second marketing campaign of deception is far more subtle and dangerous. If people recoil from the notion that "There's probably no God," then where will they go? Perhaps they'll head in the general direction of believing in a Creator. If they are not too particular about the direction they go, they may develop some form of believing in God in a generic, politically correct sense and would thus consider seeking the Kingdom of God to be a reasonably worthy pursuit. If they follow mainstream culture, this somewhat rudderless drift toward God could actually take them into currents where they should not travel.

These mainstream "dangerous" waters are found in the New Age movement and a growing post-modern philosophy within certain segments of the church itself. This undertow emphasizes the need to address major social issues from feeding the poor, prevention of disease such as the spread of AIDS, and environmental concerns including a concern about global climate change. These are all worthwhile issues to pursue, and there is much synergy in the fact that it can be embraced by virtually all forms of religion. These movements promote the concept of the Kingdom of God and creating that Kingdom here on earth by initiating efforts on improving the quality of life for all of humankind. Once again, these are noble goals, but the focus becomes more of a social agenda versus a salvation agenda.[2] It's a hedge bet. For those that felt a twinge of worry or angst about "There's probably no God", these positive efforts appear soothing to the soul. They should be careful. Satan is singing them a lullaby.

The Great Commission for all Christians is to preach the Gospel to all nations about the saving grace of Jesus Christ. This is the foremost objective, and all other pursuits pale in comparison. Jesus Christ is the antidote to our sinful nature and only He gives us the cure. He is the hope of glory. To reject Christ is to reject the One Who sent Him, which is God the Father. Contemplate the extreme for a moment. If it were possible to enable every human on earth to have enough food and supplies, to be healthy and safe from harm, yet not have Christ, then all would be lost. It would be better to suffer every day on earth with Christ than have the whole world and be without Him, for what profit is there to gain the whole world and lose your soul?

Any effort without Christ is without merit. As Jesus said Himself, "I am the vine, you are the branches; he who abides in Me and I in him, he bears much fruit, for apart from Me you can do nothing" (John 15:5 NASB).

Satan's deception is to lead mankind to pursue a noble goal without the most noble of all—Jesus Christ. He is the source of all good fruit. Unless people realize this, they will be deceived. For a general movement with such a positive social agenda has mass appeal. All can agree upon its message, and it could easily lead to a unifying and perhaps a universal religion whose central tenets are simply, "love one another" and "be good caretakers of our planet." The whole concept seems like a winner, doesn't it? What if the whole world could embrace such a concept? Wouldn't it make all our lives better?

It's a great plan of future deception. Like a wrestling or jujitsu move where you use your opponent's own momentum or inertia to flip them over, Satan can use such a positive "movement" to flip people away from the true God and His plan of salvation through His Son. Think about all the world's religions slowly unifying in thought and heading toward this common goal of ending poverty, starvation, disease, and environmental destruction. It's a worthwhile objective, and it complies with political correctness. Such a movement could gain significant momentum in a hurry, especially if the world economy is in trouble. People will want to help create solutions and do their part. The more people gravitate toward and join this global quasi-religious movement, the more momentum it will have. On the surface, it would have a very positive benefit for the world. Now here's how Satan will take this positive movement and flip it. Imagine Christians standing up and claiming that the root of our problems is sin and that we must accept Christ and Christ alone as our Savior. Would such claims be considered inclusive or divisive? Would Christians be welcomed or ostracized?

Satan will gladly give ground to a positive social agenda if he can minimize or better eliminate the emphasis on Christ.[3] It was Christ Who defeated him on the cross. Now, he will try to use a positive movement with good intentions to lead people away from the only source of their salvation. A sound social agenda of aiding the poor and the sick, loving your neighbor, and being good stewards of our planet is a wonderful objective. This is only the second half of the greatest commandment. The first half is to love God with all your heart, mind, body, soul, and strength. We cannot love God if we ignore His Son. This wonderful agenda should be done through the power of Christ, not in place of Him.

In his letter to the Colossians, Paul stated the proper attitude and approach:

> Our goal is to live a life worthy of the Lord and to please Him in every way: bearing fruit in every good work, growing in the knowledge of God, being strengthened with all power according to His glorious might so that you may have great endurance and patience, and joyfully giving thanks to the Father, who has qualified you to share in the inheritance of the saints in the kingdom of

> light. For He has rescued us from the dominion of darkness and brought us into the kingdom of the Son He loves, in Whom we have redemption, the forgiveness of sins. He is the image of the invisible God, the Firstborn over all creation. For by Him all things were created: things in Heaven and on earth, visible and invisible, whether thrones or powers or rulers or authorities; all things were created by Him and for Him. He is before all things, and in Him all things hold together (Col. 1:10–17 NIV).

Christ holds the world together. He holds this whole universe together. Any effort or objective no matter how wonderful in appearance is worthless without Christ. Do not be deceived. Whatever we do, we should be centered on Him. Jesus Christ is our All in All. He is the Way and the Truth and the Life. Believe in that truth and it will set you free. The consequences of not believing and accepting this truth are absolutely devilish.

26. Price Is Right

Many of you may recall the movie starring Robert Redford, Demi Moore, and Woody Harrelson entitled *Indecent Proposal.* In it, Moore and Harrelson play a recently married couple and Redford a wealthy businessman who offers the couple a million dollars to spend one night with Harrelson's wife, Demi Moore. Another Hollywood saga addressing the age-old question: *does everything have a price*?

More recently, many would say that indecent proposals have been made in our nation's capital. The civility between political parties is virtually non-existent, and the nation seems more divided than ever. We've got the federal government suing a state over their enforcement methods against illegal immigration. We've got states suing the federal government over government-mandated healthcare. What kind of operation have we got going here? This is no way to run a country.

At home we citizens hear the legislative rumors, and you already know it's going to be bad when the backroom deals bear names such as the Louisiana Purchase, the Cornhusker Kickback, or the Union Tax-less Cadillac. In theory, a good bill would have broad appeal and not be a coerced party-line vote. Wouldn't it be nice to have representatives who considered their integrity and moral standing to be Job Number One? Wouldn't it be comforting to know that your representatives had our country's best interests at the forefront of their minds? Wouldn't it be wonderful if our representatives put the people of this nation and their district ahead of their party and their personal political ambitions? Based on the actions and behavior of many of our elected officials, it seems that Washington's answer to these questions is, as Aerosmith would say, "Dream On."

Perhaps it is too convenient to look the other way or to dismiss such inappropriate actions as being the norm. Politicians will be politicians. Standing up for what is right is rarely easy whether you're under the intense scrutiny as an elected official or making decisions in everyday life. So what's the price? What cost would you incur to maintain your integrity? Do you avoid the shade in your business dealings or is there an illegal gap in your GAAP (Generally Accepted Accounting Principles)? Are you faithful in your marriage? Do you bend the rules like a Gumby doll when doing your taxes? How firm would you stand to protect your good name and integrity?

About 2,600 years ago, such a moral dilemma occurred and is recorded in the third chapter of the book of Daniel. Many of you are familiar with it. It's a story of three young men who faced a simple choice with immense consequences—Shadrach, Meshach, and Abed-nego. The king they faced was the great king of Babylon, Nebuchadnezzar.

King Nebuchadnezzar had conquered Judea and taken the people captive. As a practice, he took many of his best-and-brightest captives, submitted them to reeducation programs, and then brought them into his court. Shadrach, Meshach, and Abed-nego were three Hebrews taken into captivity and retrained for the king's service. They had performed well and had been promoted as officials and administrators over the province of Babylon itself.

The king decided to erect a 90-foot gold statue befitting his ego and created a rule that when certain music played, everyone would bow down and worship the golden image. If anyone did not do so, they would be thrown into a furnace of blazing fire.

The music was played and the people all worshipped—except for Shadrach, Meshach, and Abed-nego. They were brought before

Nebuchadnezzar. The king, though enraged, must have liked these three, for he gave them another opportunity to comply just in case they didn't get the memo. He said to them, "I will give you one more chance to bow down and worship the statue I have made when you hear the sound of the musical instruments. But if you refuse, you will be thrown immediately into the blazing furnace. And then what god will be able to rescue you from my power?" (Dan. 3:15 NLT).

Cut!

Now, let's bring you in as a Hebrew stunt double. Here's the scene: You're an influential administrator over the capital city of the most powerful empire of the world. It's a great job, the pay is generous, the food and amenities are excellent, and you get to hang out and rule with a couple of good buddies. Life is more than just good—it's real good. True, you've got a highly arrogant, egotistical king as a boss, and he's a bit spun up at the moment: the vein on his forehead sticks out like a Klingon warrior's. He wants to show everyone who's boss, and all you have to do is quickly bow down to this goofy golden statue. Then you're done with it, everyone can move on, and it's back to the good life. Otherwise, it's over rover; you're furnace-bound to become administrator *au flambeau.*

Now—*Action!*

What would you do? Would you *bow* to the pressure?

Since most of us would blow our lines under such a fiery scenario, let's go back and take a seat. We'll reinsert the original cast and learn from the professionals. Here's how Shadrach, Meshach, and Abed-nego responded:

> "O Nebuchadnezzar, we do not need to defend ourselves before you. If we are thrown into the blazing furnace, the God whom we serve is able to save us. He will rescue us from your power, Your Majesty. But even if he doesn't, we want to make it clear to you, Your Majesty, that we will never serve your gods or worship the gold statue you have set up" (Dan. 3:16–18 NLT).

How's that for a response to a literal trial by fire?

It certainly didn't appease the king; as that Klingon vein glazed purple and doubled in size. He ordered the temperature of the furnace increased seven-fold, and he had guards tie up the hands and feet of the three. When they opened the furnace door, the flames leaped out and killed all the guards and Shadrach, Meshach, and Abed-nego, still tied up, fell into the furnace. Then King Nebuchadnezzar leapt to his feet in amazement and asked his advisers, "Weren't there three men that we tied up and threw into the fire?" They replied, "Certainly, O king." He answered and said, "But I see four men unbound, walking in the midst of the fire, and they are not hurt; and the appearance of the fourth is like a son of the gods" (Dan. 3:24–25 NLT).

> Nebuchadnezzar then approached the opening of the blazing furnace and shouted, "Shadrach, Meshach, and Abed-nego, servants of the Most High God, come out. Come here." So Shadrach, Meshach and Abed-nego came out of the fire. Then the high officers, officials, governors, and advisers crowded around them and saw that the fire had not touched them. Not a hair on their heads was singed, and their clothing was not scorched. They didn't even smell of smoke. Then Nebuchadnezzar said, "Praise to the God of Shadrach, Meshach, and Abed-nego. He sent His angel to rescue His servants who trusted in Him. They defied the king's command and were willing to die rather than serve or worship any god except their own God" (Dan. 3:26–28 NIV).

Even an arrogant king can recognize the actions of the true God. Nebuchadnezzar then declared, " Therefore I decree that the people of any nation or language who say anything against the God of Shadrach, Meshach, and Abed-nego will be torn limb from limb, and their houses will be turned into heaps of rubble. There is no other god who can rescue like this." (Dan. 3:29 NIV).

Well, that turned out all right.

When you're with God, it always does. Wouldn't it be great if our government leaders behaved with such integrity and devotion to the God we ask to bless this nation? Let's try to elect some leaders like this. When we say, "God bless America," our leaders and we citizens should mean it, and our attitude and behavior should fully align with our request.

There is a consequence to every decision that we make, and thus everything in a sense has a cost or a price. There are some things, however, that money cannot buy, some things that money shouldn't buy, and there are some things that you should never sell.

There is a price to pay for being a follower of Christ. We all must pick up our cross and follow Him. We should always look past the cost and focus on the reward. God advertises His rewards program through His Word found in the Bible. It is the ultimate Truth in advertising, and His benefits package is so incredible that "No eye has seen, no ear has heard, and no mind has imagined what God has prepared for those who love Him" (1 Cor. 2:9 NLT).

So, speaking of Adonai advertising, we'll conclude with this compelling Christian commercial message:

Honoring the newborn King:	gold, frankincense, or myrrh
Price to convert a rogue disciple to a traitor:	thirty pieces of silver
Having the Son of God die for you in payment for all your sins:	priceless

There are some things that our money can buy; the most important thing however, has to be obtained through grace—amazing grace—how sweet the sound.

27. Driving Range

John Weber, the pastor of Christ our Shepherd Lutheran church where I had just started attending was teaching a class to new members. He was addressing the root cause of our troubles here on this earth. The class he was teaching was on the topic of sin. He wrote the word on the board as follows:

s I n

The basic problem of sin is our overemphasis on the "I." As stated before, when it comes to sin, the "I's" have it. It's a focus on ourselves from our perspective and our priorities. In our fallen state, we start out that way. It's embedded within our corrupt nature. We can blame it on Adam, but it doesn't change our status: we begin life in this world self-centered, and some of us never grow out of it.

God knows our condition. He is perfectly holy and we are not. We are spiritually separated from God and cannot have a relationship with Him in our present condition because having a relationship requires a connection, a bond. Someone perfectly holy cannot connect with someone unholy without affecting His perfect Holiness. When confronted with perfect holiness, the unholy gets obliterated. As imperfect beings, we'd be like a bug hitting a bug zapper—and we'd be zapped. But God loves us and He desires a relationship with us. He loves us so much that He gave His only Son to die for us so that whoever believes in Him shall not perish, but have eternal life (John 3:16). Through Christ, we can have a relationship with Holy God.

When we accept Jesus Christ as our Lord and Savior, then our entire relationship with God changes. "Therefore, there is now no condemnation for those who are in Christ Jesus" (Rom 8:1 NIV) and through Christ's death on the cross, we are presented "holy in God's sight, without blemish and free from accusation" (Col 1:22). All our sins are blotted out, and He forgets them completely. God now sees us as holy thanks to Jesus, and therefore we can come into His presence and have a direct relationship with the Father.

So what about sin? Well, we can still screw up. From the believer's perspective, sin is like a bad golf shot. In most cases, we recognize it right away. Sometimes, we even suspect that we're lined up wrong, but we swing at the ball anyway. The results are predictable. Depending upon your level of self-control (a fruit of the Spirit), you may immediately vocalize in colorful language your opinion of the outcome, but in a short time, you regain your composure; rethink the mechanics and your swing thoughts, evaluate what went wrong, and then make the appropriate adjustments. The next step, as most golfers will tell you, is crucial: *Learn from it,* then *forget about it,* and *focus on your next shot.* Dwelling upon your mistake will cloud your mind and attitude, and it will adversely affect your game. Dwelling upon a sin once you've repented and made amends for the damage you caused serves no purpose either. God remembers them no more, so why should you?

For both believers and nonbelievers, there are consequences to our bad shots (sins) in life. From the worldly prospective, your errant shot may end up with a difficult lie that you must deal with. But here's the good news for those who have accepted Christ as Savior: God doesn't count the stroke against you. Your sins (or excess strokes) are forgiven. Through the amazing grace of our Lord, you get unlimited Mulligans. When Christ died for us on the cross, all our sins were forgiven. Every sin we have committed, are committing, and ever will commit are washed clean from His shed blood. How's that for a loving and gracious Father? That while we are yet sinners, Christ died for us (Rom 5:8) and has cleansed us from all unrighteousness (1 John 1:9).

If you're not a golfer, then use a car expense account analogy. In our journey through life, anytime we sin, there's a vehicle expense. With Christ, we have an unlimited budget and He picks up the tab.

"Well, holy blank check!" we might say. "Whether on the golf course or on the road, let's just drive however we want."

Hold on there, tiger. Think about this a moment. Driving however you want is the "secret agent in disguise" methodology. That's where you say that you are a believer in Christ, yet your actions speak otherwise. You go around and introduce yourself: "The name's Bondage. James Bondage—license to sin."

Is that the smart way to play? Virtually all of us golfers do not tee up our ball and intentionally drive it into the woods. We do that enough without trying. If you had a really nice car (Ferrari, Bentley, Lamborghini, AC Cobra, or Corvette), would you trash it just because you can afford to have it repaired? Most would say no. Well then, to go on living in sin when you have accepted Christ as your Lord doesn't make any sense either.

During my last tour of duty in the U.S. Navy, an Air Force major friend of mine and I traveled together to teach a class on military logistics at the U.S. Marine base in Albany, Georgia. One evening as we headed out to dinner, she asked me an interesting question that some of you may have heard before: "If you were on trial for being a Christian, would there be enough evidence to convict you?"

After a moment of contemplation, I replied, "Yes, if the court could see my heart." She thought this was a great answer, yet I felt inwardly embarrassed by it. I immediately recognized my inconsistency. At the time I still had a significant amount of carnality in my Christian way of life. Her question served as a mirror for me to see myself. Why would I believe in Christ, yet be so easily seduced by the call of the wild? The Holy Spirit provides conviction often in unusual circumstances. My spirit was willing, but my flesh was weak and I had no real intent for an exercise plan to make it any stronger. I had no doubt that Jesus Christ was the Son of God Who died for me, but I was pretty much driving however I wanted. I was James Bondage and subsequently, I spent a fair amount of time in the rough.

There are many reasons why we can be in secret-agent-for-Christ mode. Perhaps the most common is all the distractions of the world. Busyness is the enemy of intimacy. It's tough to have a close relationship with the Father and a strong prayer life when you have a hard time getting Him on the calendar. In addition to this, without being deeply rooted in Christ, the lure of the world can overwhelm our old sinful nature. Even the wisest man of all, Solomon, eventually succumbed to this temptation by having his heart led astray. Of course, he had 700 wives and another 300 mistresses (concubines) to deal with. If trying to love two women is like a ball and chain (as the Oak Ridge Boys sang), then trying to love a thousand must be like having the planet Jupiter strapped to your leg.

Another reason we can be in secret agent mode is not studying His Word in the Bible. Right after I finished college in 1983, I was sworn in as a Navy officer and attended the Navy Supply Corps School in Athens, Georgia. One day we had finished a class a few minutes early and the class of about thirty student officers starting talking about an important topic---football. One student brought up the point that he saw on several occasions someone holding up a sign, "John 3:16" and wanted to know what that was. Only one person in the class knew what the verse said. Only *one* out of thirty and I wasn't that person. It wasn't because of my upbringing. Our family went regularly to church. It was a Lutheran church and if you're familiar with that type of service, it is very structured. Lutherans are like the teenage version of Catholics.

The service has a lot of repetition of sayings, confession of sins, standing up, sitting down, kneeling, standing back up---if you threw in some ab crunches, you'd have a Pilates class. There are tons of scripture quoted repeatedly week after week and none of it stuck. I could repeat the sayings, but I didn't even know that it was verses of scripture because I was not studying His Word.

Paul's second letter to Timothy states that "All Scripture is inspired by God and is profitable for teaching, for reproof, for correction, for training in righteousness" (2 Tim. 3:16 NASB). God's book is to be read on a routine basis and not serve as a static display on a tabletop or shelf. It's the playbook for living life well, and ignorance of it will cause you to have a faith a mile wide and an inch deep. Such a shallow knowledge of God's instructions and principles makes one vulnerable to deception.

The most difficult aspect of secret agency to overcome is one's level of commitment. God is not looking for part-time employees. He wants His followers to be "all in," 24 hours a day, 7 days a week. Christianity is not a religion, but a way of life centered on a relationship with the Creator of the universe. It's a methodology of the heart. When we remove the "I" from the center of our lives and replace it with Christ, then we have the proper alignment and perspective that God desires. Some grasp this rather quickly, while most of us take years to figure this out. The theory and logic are not too hard to grasp. God knows all and can do all. He loves you far more than anyone else. He knows what is best for you and wants what is best for you. Therefore, you can choose to follow His advice and direction or go out and wing it on your own. If you choose your own path, He is patient with you. Sooner or later you'll get tired of constantly playing from a bad lie. It took a lot of poor golf shots for me to figure this out. Hopefully, you'll catch on sooner. The grass is greener and nicer in the fairway and when you dedicate your life to following Him, you'll spend a lot more time there.

If we have Christ at the center of our lives, will we hit 'em straight and make lots of birdies and even soar (score) like eagles? When you have Christ at the center of your life, it's like having the wisest caddy living within you, leading you through every shot. So yes, you will score very well. There will still be times when you hit a shot down the middle, and it takes a bad bounce or ends up in a divot. God challenges and tests those He loves so that they will be better and more fruitful in their game. In the end, however, you will be pleased with your score. Looking back you will recognize that having Christ at your center was not just the fair way, but the only way to play.

28. This Is a Test

Stephen Ministry is a program where lay personnel (Blue Collar faith walkers) have been trained and are supervised in providing one-on-one care to individuals going through an emotionally difficult situation or crisis. A typical scenario is that the Stephen Minister will spend about an hour or more a week providing support with his or her "care receiver" in a spiritual walk together through the care receiver's season of difficulty.

I became a Stephen Minister about five years ago. When I first signed up for the program, I really didn't know what to expect. Most of the training made logical sense until we got to the methodology. Here we were told that it was a process-oriented methodology, not a results-oriented methodology.

At that point I said, "Whoa! Hold it! Time out…We're here to help these people through their problems, right? Aren't we looking for good results? Let me help out as I'm a consultant. I'll explain to you how business world 'best practices' problem-solving works. First you define the problem you are facing. Then you assess your current situation. This is called the *As Is* or *Current State*. Then you envision where you want to be. This is your *To Be* or *Future State*. The final step is to develop a plan or roadmap of the set of tasks, milestones, and objectives necessary to get you from your Current State to your Future State. Then it's just, 'Get 'er done.'"

As I soon discovered, the Stephen Ministry is nothing like that.

The first thing you realize in Stephen Ministry is that you are just the helper; God is the Healer. You're just the vessel; you're just the conduit for His love, mercy, and grace to flow through to meet the care-receiver's needs.

Learning this methodology has been one of the greatest blessings in my life. As a Stephen Minister, I have had the privilege of a front row seat watching the hand of God work in someone else's life. As Bob Uecker would say, "I'm up on the front row." Of course there was prayer and preparation before each weekly meeting, but once our sessions got into the groove, you could sense the Holy Spirit leading the interaction. It got to a point where I would just have the attitude of "Let's break out the popcorn and see what God is going to do next."

It's not about following a set of tasks or meeting a bunch of milestones and deliverables. It is simply having a listening ear, a compassionate heart, and taking your care-receivers' hands and helping them reestablish their grip into the hand of Jesus Christ. When you trust in the Lord with all your heart, and lean not on your own understanding (for that understanding can get real cloudy under very stressful situations), He will direct your path and He will get you through the valley that you are in.

Let's consider the big picture for a moment. Today, you don't have to be a prophet to see the dark clouds out there on the horizon. They are already overhead. Our country is going through a difficult time right now and it probably will get worse—in some scenarios a lot worse. Our circumstances are a much deeper problem than just a financial crisis, high unemployment, and oil gushing in the Gulf. There is a spiritual battle going on for our nation's soul.

But we Christians should not cower in fear. In fact we should do the opposite and stand up, close ranks, put on the full armor of God, and get in the game. We need to pray for our nation, look after our neighbors, and help out our "shipmates." We should "bear one another's burdens and thereby fulfill the law of Christ" (Gal. 6:2 NASB). There are forces within our nation that are either naively or intentionally leading us away from what makes America great. We need to rally our brethren in Christ, promote the Gospel, and get our nation in a position so that God can bless us. That position is on our knees in prayer.

God did not give us a spirit of fear. He gave us a spirit of power and of love, and love never fails. God never fails. If God is for us, then who cares who's against us? ("Hey, I choose Jesus…Devil, you can take as many draft picks as you want.") With Christ, we're already on the winning team. That's not just in the next life, but in this life right here, right now.

Knowing all that, however, doesn't make the road we're traveling on any less bumpy. The reason we call it a tough time is because it's tough. We all are going to have to face trials and tests in our lifetime. That's inevitable. Through God's Providence that we don't fully understand, some of us will face a much more difficult exam than others.

There are typically two distinct responses that we have when facing adversity. We either become better or bitter. Unfortunately, we seem to parallel the rules of the English language where it is "i" before "e," and our initial default response is that we become bitter. We ask, "Why me, Lord?" Then we wallow in replaying scenarios of what could have been instead of what currently is.

Like the English language however, there is an exception to the rule. It is *"i"* before *"e"* except when following *C*. When you follow *C*, when you follow Christ, it is *"e"* before *"i."* When faced with a difficult trial—you get better.

One of the most difficult tasks as a Christian is to heed the advice of James and "consider it all joy" when we face trials. It requires a lot of trust to grasp that what you are going through is glorifying God and increasing your capacity to produce good fruit. The Apostle Peter encourages us to persevere:

> …though you may have had to suffer grief through many trials. They have come so that your faith—of greater worth than gold, which perishes even though refined by fire—may be proved genuine and may result in praise, glory and honor when Jesus Christ is revealed" (1 Peter 1:6b–7 NIV).

Our Lord promises us that He will never leave us or forsake us. We can cast our burdens upon Him, and He will sustain us through whatever circumstance we face. That is a great comfort and gives us that peace of mind that passes all understanding even in the most difficult of storms. We must anchor our heart in that promise. When we do, we can go forward in whatever situation, confidently knowing that when we walk with the Lord, He will get us over every hill and through every valley that we face. We can do all things through Christ, Who strengthens us.

29. My Lord

Jeff McAdams

He came to earth one glorious night
The Morning Star aglow;
And gloried in the Father's will,
To Calvary He did go.

He did not have to die for me,
Of this I fully know;
But yet He died upon the cross,
So many years ago.

And though He died He lives again,
To Heaven He did go;
But soon He'll come in glory bright,
To crush the evil foe.

I've sinned against a Holy God,
And fallen oh so low;
And though I've lived a life of sin,
His mercy doth He show.

My sins are covered by His blood,
His grace doth overflow;
My Lord and Savior Jesus Christ,
Oh how He loves me so.

30. A "Soul" Purpose

Lela Battistini

Sitting at my computer, controlling the urge to throw it across the room, I am interrupted once again. For starters, my computer is so slow that it could be going backwards. On top of that, every page I try to load says, "server not found." How can that be when I know I have an Internet connection? So I close out of Mozilla Firefox, let it rest for a minute, then pull it up again. It will work, but only for a short period of time. So I close out again, unplug it from the router and modem, and count to ten. I do this because the manual says to and because if you're angry, you're supposed to take a deep breath and count to ten. So this is what I did, several times over the previous couple of days. I am using a desktop, but I know it can be throwable.

As soon as I get it working and I think I'm on a roll, I get interrupted. My children are fighting or it's time to take them to Vacation Bible School or pick them up. I have to go clean a house, or the phone rings, or I have to change our Webelos camping trip plans, or somebody is hungry. The last straw for me tonight was having my son, who should have been in bed, come to me at the desk and ask me a question. Remember, I am already frustrated, angry and think there are way too many Scripture quotes in this book that I am working on.

I am the unofficial editor of this book before it goes to the real editor. I am referencing Bible quotes, to denote the translations used (NIV, NLT, etc.) as a writer cannot simply put book, chapter, and verse. I am also checking for spelling and grammatical errors and highlighting any changes. It is tedious, challenging, and time-consuming work. When the computer won't cooperate, it is maddening as well. I am to the point of giving up for the night, but I am on deadline…and then my nine-year-old son Casey appears at my side.

I turn to him and tell him to go to bed.

He says he has a question.

I say, "Fine, what is it?"

He replies to me in a nervous, swaying way, "What is sin?"

I gape at him. I wasn't expecting that. I thought it was a delay tactic to keep from going to bed. I have learned to just let my kids say what they've got to say, and then send them back to bed, instead of saying, "Go to bed." It eliminates a repeat performance of coming back and trying to ask whatever question they think is so important. But this one threw me for a loop.

The kids have been going to Vacation Bible School all week, so I asked him if this was what he was learning there.

He said, "Yes," so I pulled up the Ten Commandments through Google. I did not have trouble with loading that page. I read them to him one by one and tried to explain, in kid language, what each commandment meant. He then tried to interpret what I was saying by repeating it in his own words. I would correct him, and I definitely told him Transformers had *nothing* to do with it. Bumblebee and Optimus Prime weren't involved.

But in his mind, they might be. He asked, "When Optimus Prime said to Bumblebee that one of the Transformers shouldn't die in vain, was that what one of the commandments meant?"

Well, sorta. I explained that *in vain* meant *for no purpose.* "To use God's name in vain," I said, "means to use it for anything other than praising Him."

Whew. We made it past the Ten Commandments. He then told me he was playing the angel in the burning furnace.

I said, "There is no burning furnace." Okay, duh me. I was thinking modern technology, not biblical times. They didn't have home furnaces back then.

He kissed me goodnight and walked away.

Lo and behold, the next story I started editing, as soon as he walked away, was the story of Shadrach, Meshach, and Abed-nego. I didn't fall out of my chair, but it was close. I called him back into the room, and I said all those names and the king's.

He said, "I can't pronounce their names, but that is the story."

I said, "You get to play God's angel in the fire?"

He said yes. So I read him the story.

By golly, it said "furnace." We went back to the Ten Commandments where the one says do not worship statues and false gods. I explained that this is what God was talking about. The king was so important to himself that he had a statue made, and he wanted everyone to bow before it. Those three guys said, "No," because they would only worship the one true God, so they were thrown into the furnace. However, an angel of God walked with them and protected them.

I told him there is only one God and only one Jesus, and that if He lives in our hearts we are saved. I told him God is everywhere, and when he began looking around the room for God, I explained that He was invisible.

He asked me where everywhere was, so I said, "In our hearts."

Casey told me he wanted to go to Heaven by going to where Jesus died and climb the bridge to shake hands with God. (Not sure where this came from.) He asked where Jesus had died, and I told him Jesus died in Jerusalem. I told him there is no literal bridge to Heaven, and the only way to get there is to believe that Jesus is the Son of God. You should live your life making God happy and when you die, God welcomes you into Heaven.

Now, tell me God doesn't work in mysterious ways? I haven't had any problems with my computer since then, either.

I told Tom (the creator of *Blue Collar Faith*) that I didn't have any stories to share to include in this book. I didn't want to think of any, and some things I just don't want to remember but my son Casey opened my eyes with his childlike wonder of all that is holy and just. We should all seek Him with such innocence. It reminds us that we adults need to do more than brush up on our Scripture to answer questions during Vacation Bible School. We need to incorporate Scripture into our daily lives—myself included. I recognize the fact that I am doing this for a reason. Even though I have obstacles impeding my progress, somebody, somewhere is learning the Word of God. Tonight it was me, through my son's innocent question and his "soul" purpose for still being awake.

31. Lord of the Rings

How did we sports fans ever survive without instant replay? One could only guess the number of games where the outcome would have changed had the inclusion of this modern video technology been available. Many "purists" would argue against having instant replay as it slows down the game and interrupts the flow. There's also the psychological effect on the referees—do they try harder because they are now more scrutinized, or do they relax because they have replay as their backup?

No matter what your opinion of instant replay, you must admit that the goal is noble. It's not about political correctness and appeasing the home crowd, nor increasing network ratings by keeping the game close (although many fans suspect this when a call doesn't go their way). The goal is to discover the truth—what truly happened on the play in question. Did the receiver have the ball, was the serve in or out, or did the clock run out before the shot? Inquiring minds want to know.

Seeking the truth is never a waste of time. Knowing the truth is a valuable asset. Understanding the truth opens doors to opportunity. Truth is the universal measuring stick in how we should evaluate our circumstances and make our decisions.

What is truth? Ironically, Pilate asked that very question to Jesus—the very One Who is Truth. He was looking at Truth, speaking to Truth, and he didn't even know it. In this earthly life, we will never know the full truth about everything. That would require omniscience. Yet there is one truth that you should grab hold of and hang onto with all you have: Jesus Christ is Lord. He is God's Son, the Light of the world, the Savior of the world, and He is the Way (to act), the Truth (to believe), and the Life (to live). Everything else pales in comparison to this fundamental truth. It is the cornerstone of Christian faith. It is Truth.

You can debate the merits of sprinkling versus full immersion in baptism. You can ponder the mystery of communion—does Christ enter the bread and wine when the priest rings a bell (Catholic), enter upon consumption (Lutheran), or is the bread and wine simply symbols to remind us of the body and blood of Christ (Baptist)? You can even quibble about where to draw the salvation line. It is by faith alone, yes, but faith without works is dead (or not legitimate faith). Therefore should you move it an infinitesimal smidge toward some type of "work" that validates their faith? These are worthwhile topics to consider, but the most important thing is simply to accept Jesus Christ as Lord.

We can move a few hours forward from when Pilate spoke to Jesus to another man who spoke to Jesus. We don't know his name, only that he was a criminal and he was being crucified beside our Lord. We do know what he said, and we recognize that through God's amazing grace, he saw the Truth. In a humble confession of repentance, he said, "Lord, remember me when you come into your kingdom" (Luke 23:42 AKJV). That's all it took. Jesus confirmed this when He replied, "I tell you the truth, today you will be with me in paradise" (Luke 23:43 NIV).

There was no baptism. There was no breaking of bread and sharing wine. There were no good deeds—it's a little difficult to accomplish anything when you're nailed to a cross. It was simply a genuine, heartfelt recognition of the Lordship of Jesus.

So does this mean that we pause for a moment, say those nine words, and then go back to our regularly scheduled program already in progress? Of course not. Accepting Christ is a life-altering event. Following Christ is a lifelong journey of dedication. You pick up your cross and follow Him. This is not a punishment; this is a blessing, for His yoke is easy and His burden is light. All who are heavy laden will find rest in Him. It's a journey of peace and true fulfillment. We serve Him out of honor and love. We worship Him and give glory to Him because He is fully entitled to it. Baptism is our public statement of our lifetime commitment to Christ. When we take communion, we reflect on His overwhelming sacrifice and His love and His grace that He bestows upon us. We do this in remembrance of Him.

When you accept Christ as your Savior, it's the commitment of a lifetime for a lifetime. It's also the obvious recognition that God knows best, that He loves you infinitely more than anyone else, and therefore His way and purpose for you is far better than any plan that you can conceive on your own. When you grasp the Big Picture, you recognize that though you live in this world, you are not of this world. Like those instant replay cameras, you gain a different perspective on what's going on; you gain a better insight into the truth. As you open your heart and surrender your will to Christ, your life merges with His will such that you understand what the Apostle Paul is saying when he writes:

> I have been crucified with Christ; and it is no longer I who live, but Christ lives in me; and the life which I now live in the flesh I live by faith in the Son of God, who loved me and gave Himself up for me (Gal.2:20 NASB).

In his book, *The Rest of the Gospel,* Dan Stone provides some excellent illustrations of this different perspective that Christians should have on this earthly life. It's like drawing a horizontal line. Above the line is the unseen, eternal world, and below the line is this temporal world. We live below the line, but our perspective should be from above the line. As Paul puts it in 2 Cor. 4:18 (NIV), "So we fix our eyes not on what is seen, but on what is unseen. For what is seen is temporary, but what is unseen is eternal." This is a difficult saying for left-brained people. How can we fix our eyes upon something that is not seen? How would we know that we're even looking at it? We do not use our physical eyes, but our spiritual eyes. This isn't some mystical "third eye" where you must meditate, chant, and burn incense to get it to open. It's a perspective of seeing things from God's eternal view. As John Polkinhorne describes, it's like putting on God's spectacles behind your eyes. Challenges become opportunities. A difficult trial in our life may produce suffering for us in the temporal world, but if we persevere, it gives glory to God. In the parable of the Good Samaritan, the victim of the robbers was an inconvenience to the priest and the Levite who passed him by. The Samaritan saw him as an opportunity to serve and to help a person in need. It is viewing life from a different frame of reference.

We live by faith, knowing that, "Faith is the confidence that what we hope for will actually happen; it gives us assurance about things we cannot see" (Heb. 11:1 NLT). It's the true Kingdom-of-God perspective. It gives us rest knowing that Christ is living through us and peace knowing that God is in control.

Another one of Stone's illustrations demonstrates the three aspects of the human persona. We have our physical part, our mental and emotional part (often called the psyche), and our spiritual part. Now think how this triad operates together. Try to picture three concentric rings. The outer ring is the physical. The next ring is the psyche, and the inner ring is the spiritual. Surrounding these three rings is the world or the environment in which we live.

Now, the vast majority of information comes from the environment into our physical being. It comes through our five senses. We see things, we hear things, we smell, taste, and touch things. This input goes from our outer physical ring to the second ring, which is where our mental/emotional abilities reside. Here the information is processed.

Once evaluated, information is typically sent back through the physical in the form of a response—a physical action or expression and/or verbal retort. This happens thousands of times a day. What's your spirit doing during all of this? Sometimes that "inner voice" provides a moral input. Most of the time, it's "opinion" is not even solicited.

When we accept Christ as our Savior, the Holy Spirit comes and dwells within us and becomes connected with our spirit. In 1 Cor. 6:17 (NASB), Paul writes, "But the one who joins himself to the Lord is *one spirit* with Him" (emphasis added). This is your source of strength and power.

Let's go back to the process described above. Input comes in from the senses. It goes to the mind or psyche. The next step is for the psyche to consult with the spirit and have the spirit (which is connected to His Spirit) "advise" the psyche how to direct the physical body to respond. This is how Christ lives through you.

Why does Paul advise us to "pray unceasingly" (1 Thess. 5:17) and to be "praying at all times in the Spirit" (Eph. 6:18)? First, it establishes our reliance on God. Secondly, it helps us to retrain our brain to point in the right direction. If we are in constant communication with God, the communication link between our mind and our spirit is open. We operate from a prayer-spirit communication-conscious state. The input from the world comes in through our senses, the mind receives that input, consults with our spirit, which is linked to the Holy Spirit, and then generates the proper response.

Look at our Master, Jesus. We read in the Bible how our Lord Jesus was constantly praying to the Father, and the clarity that He had of the Father's purpose for His life was flawless. Jesus communicated with the Father like a bundled T-1, line, whereas our communication is often like a faulty dial-up. In cell-speak, Jesus had four bars where we often get, "Searching for Network." He was in constant communication with the Father because His Spirit and the Father's were one.

The physical input that He received came through the same means as yours and mine. He saw and heard with human eyes and ears—the input to His brain while He was here on earth was no different than what you and I experience. The difference was His perfect communication with the Father directing Him in what to do through every step. He made this claim Himself—"I do nothing of My own, but speak just what the Father taught Me" (John 8:28), "judge as God tells Me" (John 5:30), "sees what the Father is doing and go and do also" (John 5:19), and "do exactly what My Father commanded Me" (John 14:31).

It is this reliance on the Father, this dependence on the direction and guidance from the Holy Spirit that we are to seek. When we operate from a pure heart, this communication channel becomes wide open. A pure heart is not a perfect heart; it's an honest one—a heart focused on truth. It's a heart that understands that we can trust God completely with our lives and we actively "listen" for His input to direct our actions. Jesus stated that the pure in heart will "see God" (Matt. 5:8). Jesus had a perfectly pure and sinless heart. Therefore He clearly saw from the eternal perspective what the Father was doing. We can never match the heart of Jesus, but as we purify our heart through our trust and surrender to Him, we too can gain a glimpse of that above-the-line view.

When we deviate from this process and start to rely upon ourselves by having our "I"s fill our thoughts and take priority of our direction ("I will do this" or "I want that"), we clog our communication line with the Holy Spirit. The network traffic between the spirit and mind becomes busy or even disconnected, and we often miss out on the Holy Spirit's input.

Maintaining our communication with the Spirit is a difficult "skill," for lack of a better word, for many of us to develop. First, we are bombarded in this world through our sensory input. The vast majority of all marketing and advertising is designed to appeal to our "flesh" or physical nature. Every advertising firm knows that "sex sells."

Unrestrained desire leads to coveting. The devil knows this, too. It's all very persuasive to our carnal needs. The "worries of this world" appear to scream at us for attention. It's hard to maintain a perspective from above the line when we're so immersed in the input from below the line. That's why prayer is so important. If we do not have that continuous attitude of prayer and frontal lobe focus of God's presence, then we are easily distracted.

Second, if we have an impulsive personality or have a take-charge attitude, then we have a tendency to "grab the ball and run with it," led by our own wisdom and intellect. We fail to pause to get that invaluable input from the Spirit. Though our intentions are good, we often "outrun our coverage."

It's a process. Like "total quality management" in the business world of continuous process improvement, the sanctification process in the spirit realm is the continuous pursuit of perfection—the pursuit of becoming Christ-like. It's a lifelong process. Don't overly worry about making mistakes. The Apostle Paul assures us in his letter to the Romans that "we know that God causes all things to work together for good to those who love God, to those who are called according to His purpose" (Rom. 8:28 ESV).

The Father looks after His children and He knows our hearts. If we seek His will through continual prayer and communication with His Spirit within us, then He will guide our steps. Make Jesus the Lord of your rings and the Lord of your life. You will then walk in truth, and there is absolutely no better way to travel.

32. All In

America loves a winner. This is true in all circumstances, but especially true in sports. There is a thrill in the competition itself, and fan approval occurs when both competing parties give it their all.

Coaches employ a variety of motivational techniques to get the maximum effort from their players. Catchphrases are common:

"Finish the drill!"

"Give a hundred-and-ten percent."

"Go to the bell (or whistle)."

"Hold nothing back!"

"Gut check time!"

"Leave it on the field!"

In football, almost every team holds up four fingers to denote the fourth and final quarter and claim both their ownership of the end game and their commitment to give all they've got.

It's impressive to see the level of commitment and valiant effort by the players. Even fans cheer with great enthusiasm. Doesn't it seem logical or rational that we should have the same level of commitment and enthusiasm to our faith and spiritual walk in life? Shouldn't our commitment to the Creator of the universe be a little more important than a ball game? Shouldn't our zeal for the Lord, Who gave us the ability to compete, to perform, or even just to cheer, be the greatest motivation? Without Him, everything else goes away.

It's not like these are competing or mutually exclusive events. You can serve the Lord through your commitment to excellence in sports or whatever you do. As Paul wrote to the Colossians, "Whatever you do, work at it wholeheartedly as though you were doing it for the Lord and not merely for people" (Col. 3:23 ISV).

Strangely, it doesn't seem to work this way. The investment or level of commitment toward the Lord rarely surpasses the level of commitment to worldly things. Somehow, God gets left out or is given a back seat. If you ask someone if they believe in God, most will say yes. If you then ask how that affects their behavior, then you get a few puzzled looks and a very diverse range of answers.

Aside from those who never acknowledge God at all, there appears to be three distinct strategies of an individual's commitment to their faith and spiritual walk. The first strategy is the Russian roulette method. This approach delays any sort of commitment to the Lord until the very last moment. The goal is to live your life your own way with you in control for as long as possible, with a planned conversion experience just before death. Their hero would be the one thief on the cross who asked Jesus to remember him when Jesus entered His Kingdom. He was assured a place in paradise just hours before his death. He did it his way until there were no more options—okay, he made it into Heaven, but notice that "his way" got him nailed to a cross in the first place.

The danger of this approach is that you might "kick the bucket" before conversion. Now you're cooking not with fire, but in fire. Refer to the parable of the rich fool in Luke 12:16–21, for he thought he had it made and found out he had made the biggest mistake of all.

The second approach is the Hokie Pokie. Just like the song—put your left foot in, take your left foot out, put your left foot in, and shake it all about—it's the I'm sorta committed thing. You know the type.

They range from those who show up to church on Christmas and Easter to renew their "fire insurance" to those who treat church and faith as a task to complete—a section of their pie chart of time rather than a way of life in a spiritual relationship that permeates everything they do. They thank God when things luckily go their way and pray fervently when they are in need or trouble. The rest of the relationship is managed laissez faire.

These are lukewarm Christians, and Jesus doesn't have great things to say about that way of life. Refer to John's address to the church in Laodicea in Rev. 3:14–19. where Jesus says to those who are neither hot nor cold that He will spit them out of His mouth. Not a pretty picture is it?

The last group of people is like the gamblers in the Texas Hold'em World Series of Poker where they bet all their chips and go "all in." They push all their chips out on the table on one hand. In the spiritual analogy they would also dive on top of their chips on the table and commit their entire being. It's betting all you got—what you have materially, and your heart included.

This is the attitude of heart that pleases the Lord. He is the Great Coach, and He wants us to go all out, finish the drill, and leave it on the field. The other strategies at best yield little fruit and are dangerous tactics to employ. Why do something halfway? A half-hearted commitment toward anything demonstrates a genuine lack of faith.

Jesus taught many parables about the Kingdom of Heaven, or as He sometimes phrased it, the Kingdom of God. The Kingdom of Heaven is not just about Heaven. It's also about a way of living life to its fullest here on earth. It is the first priority of what we are to pursue in life and it guarantees that all our needs will be met. "But seek first His kingdom and His righteousness, and all these things will be added [provided] to you" (Matt. 6:33 NASB).

In chapter 13 of the book of Matthew, Jesus gave two of these parables: "The Kingdom of Heaven is like treasure hidden in a field.

When a man found it, he hid it again, and then in his joy went and sold all he had and bought that field. Again, the Kingdom of Heaven is like a merchant looking for fine pearls. When he found one of great value, he went away and sold everything he had and bought it" (Matt. 13:44–46 NASB).

Notice that the approach of the main characters in these two parables is completely different. The first person was not looking for any treasure, but he discovered it. The second one was a seeker. He knew that something existed "out there" that had tremendous value. They came from totally opposite directions, the first uninformed, the second informed, but they both reached the same conclusion and made the same response. When they discovered the treasure (the Kingdom of Heaven), they sold all that they had in order to obtain it. They went "all in."

Is it worth the price? You bet your life. But don't feel bad about wondering as Peter implied his concern when he reminded Jesus, "We have left everything to follow you." (Mark 10:28 NIV). Jesus assured Peter that no one who left what they had for Him and the Gospel would fail to receive many times (100-fold) in this age and in the age to come, eternal life (Mark 10:29–30, Luke 18:29–30).

In this age of uncertain investing, there is one sure bet. Go all in—give all you have to Jesus, and you will reap an incredible return.

33. God's Own Agenda

Zoraya Valdez

While going on a missionary trip to Taiwan in the summer of 2009, I did not know what was in store for me, except that I was going to participate in the Vacation Bible School as teacher and in spreading the Gospel. My prayer was that the Lord would allow me to be one of His envoys. Even though we did not speak Mandarin or Cantonese, we communicated through interpreters with the people as they heard of Jesus and His love.

After traveling for almost twenty hours by plane and train to get to Taitug, we were happy and thankful that the Lord let us arrive in good spirits. Most importantly, I was thrilled to hear my dearest son Eliseo's voice by phone, as were the rest of my companions to hear their families when they called.

Every morning we would get up to have our group devotional and to plan our day. From there, we would go to a school to teach the Scriptures to the children of the area, as well as arts and crafts and fun games. We would spend a wonderful time with them regardless of the high humidity and the overwhelming heat that summer. At the end of our activities, we would return to plan visitation and spreading of the Gospel in the afternoons.

One particular afternoon, I was supposed to visit one of my students but instead I was assigned an unknown young man and his family.

The only information I received was that he was seventeen years old and that he had a friend singing in the praise team at the local church. I meditated over this because I just did not know what to say. It was very natural to reach out to the children who attended my Bible class through games and teachings, but this new assignment felt very awkward to me. Nonetheless, I praised God for the opportunity to be chosen for that afternoon visit. As I went to the house with one of the interpreters, I asked God to give me the right words. I also wanted to be able to minister to the family according to their needs.

We walked for approximately three-quarters of a mile. When we arrived, a very kind family welcomed us with a delicious pineapple drink. I introduced myself as Zory, and I said that I was from Mexico. They were amazed that I had come from so far away and took the time to meet them. I thanked them for the privilege of letting me share the Good News with them. I asked if any of them had ever heard of Jesus. They responded that they had never heard of Him. I said that I wanted to tell them about the story of Jesus Christ.

The lady of the house, a mother of seven boys, told me that she did not believe that God would be willing to forgive her after having abandoned her family. She had just returned to them two months prior, but there was lots of friction and resentment among them. Tobi, the second child, asked me if God loved him, and why had He permitted his mother to abandon the children to the care of the grandmother, as this had caused the children great sorrow. Such was the opening I needed to speak about forgiveness. I directed my attention to the mother and asked for the reason behind her decision to leave the family. She said that her husband abused her daily, and that he treated the family dog nicer than he treated her. She said that she had left because she felt very desperate and humiliated. I felt compassion for her. You could tell she was struggling with her situation. She was very petite and somewhat frail, being not even 5 feet tall.

When she and I finished talking, I spoke to Tobi about his mother's suffering and despair I told him that I could feel how torn her heart was after being unable to forgive herself. I told Tobi and his mother that God offers forgiveness through Jesus, and that He already paid the debt of sin. When we confess Him as our Savior, He forgives us and cleanses us. As mentioned in Isaiah, God throws our sins to the ocean and never remembers them. I told them about Christ's love, salvation, and the redeeming grace of our Lord, and that He has given us the choice of forgiveness or bitterness in our hearts. We select to live miserably and to make others' lives miserable, or we select to forgive those who affect us emotionally and psychologically. God is the only Supreme Being Who has the power to restore a suffering person when he receives Jesus as his personal Savior. I told Tobi that not only does God forgive us, but He gives us the capacity to forgive. We cannot give what we do not have. At that precise moment, the mother said that she wanted to accept Jesus to be forgiven, so we prayed together, and then with the rest of the family. It was a moving experience. Unfortunately, we then had to say our goodbyes.

When we left, the interpreter told me that she had been blessed as well with the family. We started walking down the street, back to the church where my companions were waiting for us, when suddenly I heard somebody calling "Zory! Zory!" This is how I had introduced myself to the family because it was easier than trying to pronounce my name. So, it sounded very strange that someone was calling me by my nickname in such a remote place of the earth. Again I heard "Zoryyyyy." I turned to find out who was calling me, and I saw Tobi signaling for me to wait. When he finally reached us, breathless, and panting, he could only say: "I do not know when I will see you again, maybe never, but I need your Jesus. Please give me more of Jesus." In tears, he asked me not to leave before giving him more of Jesus, and for His forgiveness for himself and to be able to forgive his mom. He did not want a bitter heart. So we hugged and cried together in the middle of the street, and that is where he was saved. We prayed, and he thanked me for giving him the Good News. How wonderful to witness the miracle of forgiveness in the hearts of that family.

It was such a happy time. At that moment, I understood that although I wanted to visit one of my students, God had a perfect plan for that family. God had a different plan than mine, because He has His own agenda. We just need to be receptive. When it was time for me to be by myself, I started praying, thanking Him for letting me be a part of such an experience, and now for allowing me to share it with you.

34. Payback

If you're a sports fan, one of the secular enjoyments of the Christmas season is the college football bowl games. These bowl games serve as a reward to those college teams that did well during the year. Though the over expansion of the bowl system has somewhat diluted that standard (teams that are just .500 can qualify), the process provides a greater benefit to a larger number of schools and their fans than would a play-off system. Besides, we still have the beloved BCS (eye roll please).

Among the many sponsors advertising during this timeframe is a large credit card company that promotes its reward system of embedding your desired photo on the credit card, having low interest rates, providing cash back, and/or awarding prizes and benefits just for being a member. Their slogan is, "What's in your wallet?" Another credit card company has a slogan, "Membership has its privileges." Both companies state that becoming a customer or member of their programs will open the door to lots of benefits and rewards that you otherwise would not have.

Did you know that God has a rewards program, too? It's true, and like the credit card companies, the rewards only apply to members. Fortunately, it doesn't have the prerequisite financial qualifications to become a member like the credit card companies demand. To become a member of God's rewards program requires no money, talent, status, or effort. It simply takes belief.

There are multiple membership clauses in the Bible: Acts 16:31a reads, "Believe in the Lord Jesus, and you will be saved"; Mark 16:16 reads, "Believe…and you will be saved"; Rom. 10:9 (NLT) reads, "If you confess with your mouth, 'Jesus is Lord,' and believe in your heart that God raised Him from the dead, you will be saved"; and, of course, perhaps the most famous, John 3:16 (NASB) says, "For God so loved the world, that He gave His only begotten Son, that whoever believes in Him shall not perish, but have eternal life."

Once you become a member, you are a member for life—everlasting life. You cannot be disqualified: "I give them eternal life, and they shall never perish; no one can snatch them out of My hand. My Father, Who has given them to Me, is greater than all; and no one is able to snatch them out of My Father's hand" (John 10:28–29 NIV).

Pretty cool, huh? Here's another commercial message—if you think you are in "good hands" with Allstate, then consider how safe you are in the hands of Jesus and the Father.

So how does this Heavenly rewards program work? We are evaluated by Christ: "For we must all appear before the judgment seat of Christ, that each one may receive what is due him for the things done while in the body, whether good or bad" (2 Cor. 5:10 NIV). It works based on our work as each will receive his own reward according to his own labor (1 Cor. 3:8). God is our cosmic CEO—He built this entire universe and all things in it are under His domain. As children of God, it's a family-owned business. We all work for Dad.

Continuing with Paul's letter to the Corinthians, he gives a building analogy similar to building up reward points for your credit card. Every time you use your card you get points. Every time you use your talents for the Lord, you get points. (1 Cor. 3:9): "For we are God's fellow workers; you are God's field, God's building" and skipping to verse 11: "For no one can lay any foundation other than the one already laid, which is Jesus Christ."

There's a reference to the membership clause again. The rewards program is based on the belief of Jesus Christ. Without that belief, you're not a member of the program, and any work performed is for nada.

So upon this foundation of Jesus Christ your membership program begins: "If any man builds on this foundation using gold, silver, costly stones, wood, hay or straw, his work will be shown for what it is, because the [Judgment] Day will bring it to light. It will be revealed with fire, and the fire will test the quality of each man's work. If what he has built survives, he will receive his reward" (1 Cor. 3:12–14 NIV).

How often have you heard that the quality of a product is based on the tools and materials that were used to make it? Well, in this scenario, you are the tool and the material is your attitude of heart. The actual accomplishment is less valuable than the attitude in which you performed it. If the work you performed is done with an attitude of selfless love, then it is purified through fire—notice gold, silver, and precious stones are refined through fire and made more brilliant. Wood, hay, straw, or actions performed with ulterior or selfish motives are consumed and destroyed. "As they are, you will suffer loss, though you yourself will be saved" (1 Cor. 3:15 ESV). This is not a salvation thing—you get your membership from your belief in Jesus Christ and you are forever in the good hands of the Father and the Son—this cannot be taken away. This is a rewards program, and actions performed with improper motives, no matter how impressive, simply do not earn points.

Later in his letter, Paul gives the ideal motivation for all action—love. In fact, he states very clearly that any action—even great and impressive things such as chatting with angels ("Hey Gabriel, how are the stars hangin'?") or predicting the future, feeding all the poor, knowing all sorts of mysteries, making huge personal sacrifices or moving mountains by pure faith—any action done without love is for naught.

Love is the essential ingredient in all action. When asked what the greatest commandment was, Jesus replied, "'Love the Lord your God with all your heart and with all your soul and with all your strength and with all your mind' and, 'Love your neighbor as yourself'" (Mark 12:30–31 NIV). If you want the Cliff Notes version of all the rules and regulations, all the "Thou shall" and "Thou shall nots" of the Bible, then this verse is it. And it has only one verb—love.

As the first sentence and key concept of Rick Warren's mega-selling book, *The Purpose Driven Life*, states, "It's not about you." It's about God as our Creator, CEO, and Father. This is His world, and He has a purpose for each and every one of us. For those who follow His program, there exists a Heavenly reward. "Let us not become weary in doing good, for at the proper time we will reap a harvest [your reward] if we do not give up" (Gal. 6:9 NIV). Invest your 401(k) program into the Kingdom of God. "Store your treasures in Heaven, where moths and rust cannot destroy, and thieves do not break in and steal" (Matt. 6:20 NLT). This is the wisest course of action.

Go back to work. Let us keep working and doing all things in love for it is not what's in your wallet, but what's in your heart that counts. Also remember that membership has its privileges, and in God's program those privileges that you have and the rewards that you earn last forever.

35. Grape Expectations

In warfare, a key component to a successful attack strategy is to quickly disrupt your enemy's command and control. Disabling or hindering their internal communication significantly reduces their effectiveness to fight in a coordinated and cohesive manner. Units will be separated or cut off from others, their command centers will not have a grasp of the "big picture," and they will lack the necessary or vital information on how to best defend themselves. Uncertainty and isolation also adversely impacts their morale, which further decreases their effectiveness in battle.

In general, avoiding isolation and maintaining good communication is a key component to successful living. In today's information age, networking is an integral part of both business and society. There are many professional Web tools such as LinkedIn that enable you to maintain business contacts, find jobs or sales opportunities, and of course there are Facebook, MySpace, and Twitter to keep you in touch with your friends.

In the spiritual realm, staying connected is absolutely crucial.

Our Lord and Savior gave us a great analogy of this, as quoted by the Apostle John in his gospel:

> I am the true vine, and My Father is the gardener. He cuts off every branch in Me that bears no fruit, while every branch that

> does bear fruit He prunes so that it will be even more fruitful. You are already clean because of the word I have spoken to you. Remain in Me, and I will remain in you. No branch can bear fruit by itself; it must remain in the vine. Neither can you bear fruit unless you remain in Me. I am the vine; you are the branches. If a man remains in Me and I in him, he will bear much fruit; apart from Me you can do nothing. If anyone does not remain in Me, he is like a branch that is thrown away and withers; such branches are picked up, thrown into the fire and burned. If you remain in Me and My words remain in you, ask whatever you wish, and it will be given you. This is to My Father's glory, that you bear much fruit, showing yourselves to be my disciples. As the Father has loved Me, so have I loved you. Now remain in my love. (John 15: 1–9, NIV)[1].

Jesus is the vine and we are the branches. He is the Source of all that we have—the ability to live life abundantly and to produce fruit for His Kingdom. We can only do this if we are connected to Him. For a branch removed from the vine can do nothing on its own, and it will eventually wither and die. To put it more bluntly, if you (a branch) are separated from Jesus (the true Vine) and planted into the ground, then you're just a stick in the mud.

The Father is the gardener who lovingly and tenderly takes care of the branches to enable them to be more fruitful. He lifts them up to get more sunlight ("Sonlight") and prunes and trims away the "wild shoots" so that the branches may grow more perfectly. As the psalmist stated in Psalm 33:13–15: "The LORD looks from Heaven; He sees all mankind. From His throne He observes all who live on the earth. He made their hearts, so He understands everything they do."

The Father knows how to dress a vine so that it becomes more productive. He knows our hearts. As we grow and become bigger and stronger, what happens to us? We begin to look more and more like the vine itself. We become Christ-like.

Jesus is the "true" vine, implying that there are others that are false. The Father is the gardener Who oversees the entire vineyard (universe). Where's the third person of the Holy Trinity? He's the Life Force flowing through us. The Holy Spirit is the sap.

Okay, so it's a good analogy, but what's the practical application for all of this? Jesus tells us to remain or abide in Him. How do we do that? We do that through worship, fellowship with other believers, prayer, and reading of God's Word. Jesus is the Word—"And the Word became flesh and dwelt among us" (John 1:14). When we read God's Word, we open up ourselves for the sap, the Holy Spirit, to flow through us and give us wisdom, inspiration, and enlightenment. As you read the Scriptures, you will have more of those "aha" moments—similar to the situation the alcoholic describes as "a moment of clarity." These insights enable you to see God's plan for you more clearly, get the proper perspective on things, and discover the correct principles to embrace.

The second part of this connection is through prayer. We should pray unceasingly in all things. Prayer is where we open up our hearts to the Father, we give Him thanks, we state our needs, and we seek His guidance. When we are spiritually reborn, we are babies in the spirit, and that has nothing to do with our physical age. You can be very old physically and yet be a spiritual infant. Like an infant we initially have lots of needs and they take priority in our lives. We focus primarily on our needs and go to God as our Cosmic Genie with our wish list. We wonder if we pray correctly and if God is even hearing us. Don't get too wrapped up in the methodology. The Apostle Paul assures us that the Holy Spirit intercedes in our prayers:

> In the same way the Spirit also helps our weakness; for we do not know how to pray as we should, but the Spirit Himself intercedes for us with groanings too deep for words; and He who searches the

> hearts knows what the mind of the Spirit is, because He intercedes for the saints according to the will of God (Rom. 8:26–27 NASB).

Don't get frustrated. Be patient. As you grow in faith, you will grow in trust and you will gain more confidence in your communication efforts and prayer life. You will migrate from the infantile "God, what will you do for me?" to the mature "God, what will you do through me?"

The last pragmatic piece is the fellowship with other believers. Hang out with your fellow branches on the vine. Get involved with your church, your Sunday school, and the various missions and ministries that they have to offer. Therefore encourage one another and build each other up (1 Thess. 5:11). Compliment their "grapes", cheer on their growth, and be encouraged by them as well. We should be like the start of the church as told in Acts 2:42 NASB: "They devoted themselves to the apostles' teaching and to the fellowship, to the breaking of bread and to prayer." Grow your network of fellow Christians; there is strength and support in numbers.

Finally, what is the fruit that we are to produce? What will abiding in the vine of Christ, tended by the Father with the sap of the Holy Spirit cruising through us, accomplish? Paul tells us in Galatians 5:22–23 NLT: "But the Holy Spirit produces this kind of fruit in our lives: love, joy, peace, patience, kindness, goodness, faithfulness, gentleness and self-control."

Don't we all want those things in our lives? To be filled with love and joy and to have patience and peace no matter what our circumstances? Wouldn't it be enjoyable to share kindness, gentleness, and goodness with others and to do it out of faithful self-control? It's an awesome way to live. When you remain in Christ, you'll produce these fruits. You may ask whatever you wish and it will be given to you. Now, that sounds like a blank check from God. However, it's not necessarily anything you want, but anything you want *in accordance with the fruits of the Spirit of abiding in Christ.* If you have desires of the flesh or your sinful nature, then they will show up as: "sexual immorality, impurity and debauchery; idolatry and witchcraft; hatred, discord, jealousy, fits of rage, selfish ambition, dissensions, factions, and envy; drunkenness, orgies, and the like" (Gal 5:19-21a). If this is your desire, then you are not a part of the true vine, and as Paul warns, "Those who live like this will not inherit the kingdom of God." (Gal. 5:21b).

Who wants to be filled with jealousy, rage, selfishness, and envy? What a stressful way to go through life. Don't let the devil disrupt your command and control and separate you from the love and spiritual nourishment of the Lord. Instead, choose a life abiding in Christ. It's the di**vine** way to live.

36. God Is in This.

Marcia Daniels

On January 12, 2010, the world stood still as Haiti experienced the most devastating earthquake known in its history. We said our prayers, gathered our composure, and continued our lives as Haitians began to dig through the rubble to find their loved ones and salvage what they could of their clothes and homes. Then the moral conscience kicked in and we began to assess the damage to determine what could be done to help thousands of mothers, fathers, families, and most of all orphaned children—children who were already orphans and those who became orphans as a result of losing their families.

Our church youth group at Bethlehem Star Baptist Church, Oklahoma City, Oklahoma, was already involved in sponsoring a child, Dachimeleck Dormainvil (Dach), through Compassion International. February 22, 2010, was Dach's birthday, and we still had no news of his whereabouts. We chose not to wait in silence but to reach out to all the children with what we called the Children–to-Children Haiti Project.

Our children decorated empty containers that previously held nutritional powder (better known as nutritional shakes) for the children in Port-au-Prince, Haiti. The cans were a perfect size for holding various sundries. We then gathered soap, wash cloths, toothpaste and brushes, candy, toy cars for the boys, and chapstick for the girls. Each gift was designed to let them know how special they are to Jesus and to us. When it came time to ship the containers, we realized there was no place in Haiti where they could be delivered, as we had no shipping address or point of contact.

Although God had already spoken to me and told me to tell Reliv, the manufacturer of those nutritional shakes, what we were doing with their cans, I did not. Instead, I listened to others' doubts and fears of sharing this information for fear it would not be received well.

Push came to shove as it often does, and I finally turned to Reliv International. I told them what we were doing with these super-sturdy Reliv cans that were relatively clean after they were used. They were very excited!

This was a relief. And yet while the news pleased Reliv International, we were still lacking a way to ship the cans to Haiti. I told Reliv about the problem. It was a Wednesday afternoon, and Reggie Ament from Reliv's Kalogris Foundation said, with excitement, "Marcia, this is God's timing."

Imagine that.

She said: "We are on our way to Port-au-Prince a week from Friday. If you can get them shipped to Kathy Brawley and Maybeeline Dungue-Despagne by Monday, we'll take them with us." I was so shocked and excited all at the same time, I could hardly contain myself.

This company had no reason to help me or our church youth with our mission project. I had already contacted several relief organizations, and they would only accept financial donations, or packages shipped a certain way.

I was very relieved that I did not have to return to our youth to tell them that we could not ship their gifts to Haiti. For more than twenty-two years, Reliv's mission has been to "Nourish the World," in mind, body, and spirit. For those who dared to believe, we learned that this is truly a company with a heart. Their mission has transcended into their everyday life so much that it is the norm.

The story only gets better from here. While our church was very capable and willing to pay the shipping, I knew that we would not be able to contact our finance department prior to the shipping date, so I called Reggie and explained our dilemma.

She said, "Marcia, just tell me how many boxes you have, and where and what time we can pick them up." Who would not want to partner with a company like this?

After all the packages were ready to be shipped, I put a bright pink heart on all the boxes because the gifts were made, shipped, and delivered with love. Reliv International agreed to ship our cans, pay the shipping, pick them up at the designated shipping location, and carry them into Port-au-Prince.

Wow. I knew God was involved, but I was still amazed when the project came full circle beyond my expectations. Reliv continued to use their resources to send our children pictures and video clips of the children receiving their individually packaged cans of goodies from children in the United States. Now our children who otherwise would not have experienced the faces and smiles of the Haitian children were able to see the rewards of their labor. To date, we still have not found Dach, but I know God is taking care of him.

Why did I second-guess the prompting of the Holy Spirit? I knew strongly in my spirit that I was to tell Reliv that we were recycling their cans in a Haiti project. Before I contacted all those other organizations, I knew I was supposed to contact Reliv, but I used my own human reasoning. When all else failed, I heard "I told you…," so I immediately called Reliv.

Reggie confirmed what I already knew, "Marcia, God is in this."

This is how God uses willing vessels to help His children. If we would just listen with our hearts and obediently follow the lead of the Holy Spirit, we can do amazing things for our world and for the Kingdom. I can only imagine how much more amazing this project could have been had I contacted Reliv first.

We must move in God's timing. God arranged for Reggie to be on her way to Port-au-Prince just in time to deliver our gifts to the Haitian children.

God is the same, yesterday, today, and forever (Hebrews 13:8). In the same way, He sent the prophet Elijah to the city of Zarephath (1 Kings 17:10) to provide for a widow and her son. However, God ordered Elijah's steps so that he arrived just in time. First, because of a severe drought in the land, He sent him eastward to the brook Cherith. There, God provided him with food, bread, and water from the brook to drink. However, after a time, God dried up the brook and He told Elijah to go to another city (v. 8). "Then the word of the Lord came to him saying, arise and go to Zarephath, which belongs to Sidon and stay there; behold I have commanded a widow to provide for you." This was God's way of providing for the widow whom He knew needed food. With God there are no coincidences. "The mind of a man plans his way, but the Lord directs his steps" (Proverbs 16:9 ESV).

When Elijah arrived, he found a widow gathering sticks for a fire so that she could prepare her last meal for her son and herself and then die (1 Kings 17: 12). Just in time, God told Elijah how to provide for her and her son. The Bible says, "She went and did according to the word of Elijah, and she and her family ate for many days" (1 Kings 17: 15).

If Elijah had argued with God, debated where God was telling him to go or what to do, the widow and her son would have died. When God is in it, He will direct the footsteps of the righteous and He will do it just in time. We have to be obedient and move as He directs us. No matter how odd things may appear, we must be obedient and move in His timing. I am so grateful that I finally called Reliv. A few days later, it would have been too late.

As for Reliv, a company does not become extraordinary on its own but it takes like-minded employees and leaders. So how did Reggie know that her organization would support this endeavor that she so eagerly embraced? It occurred to me that Reliv is the perfect example of all the old-school teachings, that leadership starts at the top and it trickles down throughout the organization. Apparently, Reliv's leaders, Robert and Sandy Montgomery, have been leading and modeling their mission, vision, and goals for the twenty-plus years that they have been in business. Reggie had already caught the vision and the mission and was running with it, delivering tents, shakes, and much more when we came along. We were another opportunity.

Some more good news: Dach, the child we were sponsoring, was later found to be safe and unharmed.

37. Who's Your Daddy? Part I

A common error made in the business world is the sense of urgency to start creating potential solutions to an issue before you've properly defined the problem. There's a sarcastic adage to this approach, "There's not enough time to do it right, but there's enough time to do it over." Trial and error, however, is typically an expensive methodology to employ.

The first step in problem solving is to accurately identify and define what the problem is. If you fail in this objective, then you end up solving symptoms of the problem that may not bring about a worthwhile solution and in many cases will make things worse. In the consulting world, one effective tool in troubleshooting a complex problem is Root Cause Analysis or 5Y as it sometimes called. It's a simple approach by asking a series of "Why" questions. Typically it takes no more than five "Whys," thus the name 5Y, to discover the root source of the problem.

Take for example this recent financial crisis. Why was there a financial crisis? Banks and financial/lending institutions were not adequately liquid to loan money to keep commerce flowing. Why were these institutions not sufficiently liquid? They had too many "toxic assets" on their balance sheets. Why did they have too many toxic assets on their balance sheets? They made too many loans to marginally or under qualified people who defaulted on their loans. Why did they make too many loans to under qualified people? The federal government relaxed lending standards and pressured these institutions to make these loans, and well, you get the picture. You keep digging until you find the root cause.

Now this is an oversimplified illustration for a complex issue, but the concept and process works just the same. Had a detailed analysis of the financial crisis been conducted, perhaps a more viable solution could have been developed than to just "throw money at it." This seems to be the standard knee-jerk reaction the federal government always makes. Unfortunately, the money we're now "throwing" at problems is not even our own. Our country is so broke that we have to borrow money from someone else to just be able to throw it. That's embarrassing.

So let's move away from inept political problem solving and tackle the most important question of all. This question has plagued mankind from the moment he had the ability to contemplate it. This is the Mother of all Root Causes. How did we get here and why are we here at all?

To tackle this problem, we'll begin by analyzing this grand universe in which we live. Let's take a look at what's going on out there and see if it has any clues. First, we'll start with a little background information. Back in the 1920s, Edwin Hubble (the astronomer that the Hubble Telescope is named after) made some startling discoveries about the stars in the sky. This discovery blew our minds with our concept of the size of the universe. It was larger—*much larger*—than we thought. The prevailing thought at that time was that our galaxy, the Milky Way, was about the extent of our universe. Hubble began to see galaxies beyond our own galaxy, and not just one, but millions of them. Millions of galaxies containing billions of stars demonstrated a huge expanse of the universe in which we live. It's really quite big.

As Hubble began to study these distant galaxies, he received some puzzling results. The light frequencies or color that he expected to see did not correspond with what he observed. What he noticed was that there was a uniform shift in the color and appearance of distant objects. Objects appeared to be more red than forecasted. This gave rise to the term "red shift" or a shifting to red end of the spectrum of light. Here's the first "Why." Why did these galaxies appear more red than expected? To interpret this phenomenon, Hubble applied the concept of the Doppler Effect.[1]

Now you NASCAR fans are very familiar with the Doppler Effect. Vocally imitate the sound of Jeff Gordon or Kyle Busch or your favorite driver's car as it goes by on the track. If there are other people in the room and they are now staring at you, do not worry. You're just following instructions. Imitate the sound again just to pique their curiosity. Notice how the pitch changes. As the car approaches, the pitch is higher and as it passes and moves away from you the pitch goes lower. This is the Doppler Effect. As an object comes toward you, it compresses the sound waves and causes them to scrunch up and be higher in frequency. As the object moves away from you, the sound waves elongate and the pitch gets lower. If you're a weather watcher fanatic, then you probably heard the weatherman talk about their Doppler radar, which tracks storms using the Doppler Effect to determine the direction the storms are heading.

Light behaves in a similar fashion. When light approaches you, it increases in frequency, and it decreases in frequency when it moves away. For visible light, higher frequencies exist in the blue and violet spectrum and the lowest frequency (longest wavelength) is red. When Hubble studied far away galaxies and noticed that the objects appeared redder than they should, this indicated that the objects were moving away. This meant that the universe was expanding. Here's the second "Why." Why was the universe expanding? Thinking backwards in time, if the universe was expanding, then the stars were closer to us last week, last month, last year, and so on. If you continue this reverse engineering long enough, you will reach a point in time where the entire universe is simply that—a point. A point of singularity where the entire universe is compressed into something that has virtually no size. We're talking way smaller than the period at the end of this sentence. That's pretty astounding.

To go back any further we end up with nothing. Now here's the final "Why." Why did the universe go from nothing to something? The answer to this folks is the Mother of all Root Causes.

We really have just two choices. The first is that we have a Creator Who pressed the cosmic start button that caused the universe to exist. The second possibility is that it just happened. Let's consider the latter solution for a moment, "It happened." This reminds me of a vulgar bumper sticker that was popular in the 1980s. It rhymes with "it happens," but I'll paraphrase here*: Poop Happens.*

There you go—the Mother of all Root Causes, the apex of scientific achievement and knowledge, the primal cause of our existence is that Poop Happens. Makes you feel good about the intellectual advancement of our species doesn't it? I wonder if the guy who coined the phrase (I'm assuming it's a guy as ladies typically don't use such language although some do when severely agitated) realized that he was formulating the ultimate theoretical answer to the ultimate human question (*Why are we here?*) and establishing the cornerstone of the philosophical and religious belief of the atheist. It's amazing what a simple bumper sticker can do. Yet several people (we will hence refer to them as Poopy Heads) subscribe to this theory. They have added complexity and various twists to the baseline Poop Theory—the Big Bang/Big Crunch theory, wherein the universe is an eternal accordion of expansion and then contraction and then expansion again, or the colliding membrane theory where multiple universes collide, or the multiple universe theory itself, but when stripped of all the extraneous postulating and tested with mathematical models, they are simply just full of poop. To dispel this theory even further, you can't even have poop without a pooper.

There is only one answer to this ultimate question: *God did it.* Even Stephen Hawking, perhaps the most brilliant scientist living today, admitted in his book, *The Theory of Everything*, "It would be very difficult to explain why the universe should have begun this way, except as an act of a God who intended to create beings like us."

It is not only the most logical answer, but it's the only answer with any logic. If you cannot see this truth, then your vision may be obscured because you have your hips on your shoulders (you may be a Poopy Head).

The pursuit of knowledge and truth has taken mankind on an incredible journey. Through the amazing achievements of science we have validated with mathematical theory and proof the origin of our universe and confirmed what theologians have known for thousands of years. The answer is contained in the leadoff sentence of His handbook inspirationally written for us: "In the beginning, God created the Heavens and the earth" (Gen. 1:1 ESV).

38. Who's Your Daddy? Part II

Science has made incredible discoveries over the past hundred years. In the last century, great strides were made both in the smallest realm of our existence, quantum physics, to the grand "big picture" of our universe through astronomy.

The scientific quest continues. In the atomic particle accelerator experiments conducted in the international CERN research center, a huge tunnel between France and Switzerland, scientists try to smash particles together to simulate the conditions of the universe when it was very young—fractions of a second old. New particles are being discovered and old ones like protons and neutrons have been broken down into smaller entities such as up quarks and down quarks. The electrons are still around, but we also have bosons, muons, tauons, and gluons. I mean, who is coming up with these names? It seems like the physics department must be downwind of the chemistry lab and is inhaling too many hallucinogenic vapors.

In astronomy, technological advancements in telescope design have enabled scientists to see galaxies at the very perimeter of our universe billions of light-years away. The expanse of this universe is incredible and awe-inspiring.

When you use a scientific eye to view how the universe was made and how it operates, you discover some statistics that are simply amazing. Below are just a few:

- Protons are 1,836 times the size of electrons. If this ratio was just a little larger or smaller, then we would not exist due to the inability of the correct molecules to form that we require for life. Likewise, if their respective charges were not exactly opposite (protons +1 and electrons -1), then we would not exist.
- Water is one of the rare molecules that expands and is less dense in solid form than it is in liquid form. This allows ice to float. Without this property, ice would sink, the earth would become a frozen ball, and life could not exist.
- Our position in our solar system and in our Milky Way galaxy is within extremely fine tolerances of the amount of heat, cold, and cosmic radiation to support life.
- If our day (rate of rotation of the earth) was either shorter or longer, if the moon was closer or further away, or if the earth's axis was tilted greater or less, then life could not exist on this planet.
- If the force of gravity was too weak, then stars would never have initiated nuclear fusion and thus create light. If too strong, stars would burn too quickly and be too erratic to support life.
- The force that holds particles together within the nucleus of an atom is called the strong nuclear force. If this force was too weak, then only hydrogen and helium would have been formed and the universe would be just space. If too strong, then mostly heavy elements would have formed and there would be not enough light elements to create life.
- The electromagnetic force is the force that bonds electrons to the nucleus. If too weak, electrons would not stay in orbit. If too strong, then electrons would not bond with other atoms. In either case, there would be no molecules.

If you were walking along a beach and you kicked up a cell phone buried in the sand, you wouldn't exclaim, "Wow, what a cool-looking rock or seashell." You would immediately recognize it as being manmade. When you look at our universe and at the life living in it, you should instantly recognize the evidence of design everywhere. Whether looking through a telescope, a microscope, or just using the naked eye, we should easily see "Made by God" stamped on everything we view. This universe is not some cosmic accident. It is not the result of an unfathomable and mathematically impossible series of random and chance events that produced life here on earth. This universe is so incredibly fine-tuned and designed to accuracies so far beyond our human capability that we all should simply stare in slack-jawed awe and marvel. When you contemplate all the intricacies involved, it is readily apparent that our universe is precisely designed to support the life that we know and experience. Paul stated this obvious observation in his letter to the Romans: "They know the truth about God because He has made it obvious to them. For ever since the world was created, people have seen the earth and sky. Through everything God made, they can clearly see His invisible qualities—His eternal power and divine nature" (Rom. 1:19–20a NLT).

Now here's the catchphrase, and it's quite condemning: "So they have no excuse for not knowing God." (Rom 1:20b NLT)

No excuse.

Why is it that there are so many people oblivious to the obvious? There are perhaps many reasons, but upon deeper analysis you'll eventually uncover the root cause—pride. Pride is a blinder to the truth and a distorter of the truth, for it disrupts the proper perspective and priority of the universe. Pride is like cataracts on your spiritual eyes. Whether it's one's pride in one's own intellect, pride in self-determining will, or pride in the ability of science or other manmade endeavors, the priority is always wrong if it does not place God first. The worst scenario is not acknowledging God at all. Any person who follows this path is walking in utter darkness.

Now here's the good news: Jesus is the Light of the world. He will bring those who follow Him out of their darkness and "to all who believe in Him and accept Him, He gives the right to become children of God" (John 1:12). Having Jesus Christ as your Lord and receiving His Spirit gives you eternal life and makes you an heir in God's Kingdom.

Further on in Paul's letter to the Romans, he states, "For you did not receive a spirit that makes you a slave again to fear, but you received the Spirit of sonship. And by Him we cry, 'Abba, Father'" (Rom. 8:15 NIV). In Galatians, Paul states virtually the same thing in verse 4:6: "And because we are His children, God has sent the Spirit of his Son into our hearts, prompting us to call out, 'Abba, Father.'"

Abba is an endearing term children use for their Father. The best English translation is *Papa* or *Dad*. That's how intimate God, the Creator of this vast and amazing universe, wants His relationship to be with His children. He wants us to call Him Daddy. Imagine that. The Creator of the universe of which materially we are just a small and insignificant piece wants to be so involved in our lives and so joined in our relationship to Him that we address Him as Father—we address Him as Dad. That's beyond humbling. He wants us to take His hand and look forward to each new day with an expectant attitude of "What are we going to do today, Daddy?"

Like little children on the playground, we can brag about our Daddy—and we can do so with absolute honesty. Our Daddy can whip anyone else's daddy, and He is the greatest Dad there is.

39. The Death of an Institution

Rick Saltzer

The word was out, the finger had written,
the box was open, the hand been bitten! –
studies completed, all findings were fair,
data dissected, no margin for error! –
analysis pure, nothing refuted,
the experts were sure, the case concluded! –

The Pillar collapsed, the Culture undone,
Tradition erased and *Chaos* begun!:

.... marches were canceled and protests recalled,
everywhere writers were "shocked and appalled" –
pundits were puzzled and poets were vexed,
media muzzled and artists perplexed –
news anchors sadly swallowed a sob,
street preachers rudely thrown out of a job –
academics took a shot to the crotch,
professors were put on suicide watch –
magazines folded and mayors resigned,
bureaucracies completely realigned –

movies and screenplays were forced to be trashed,
        the thespian world was suddenly smashed –
colleges became financially strapped,
        large chunks of valued curricula scrapped –
musicians and singers ran out of steam,
        television shows were stripped of their theme –
journalists panicked with nothing to write –
        attorneys frantically searched for a fight –
political parties were equally stunned,
        nobody could tell which victims to fund. . . .

. . . .

. . . . on that fateful day when Racism ended,
        it's safe to say confusion abounded –
the crutch on which so many depended
        gave way and left the country confounded –

a staple of everyday life removed,
        it was unclear how the people should act –
but with the new view, the nation improved,
        and the mayhem caused couldn't change that fact –

now with The Skin-Pigment Problem resolved,
        the national scene would change forever –
the Race-Based endeavors were all dissolved,
        and Colors allowed to blend together. . . .

40. That's Illogical

It's 4:30 a.m., and I am awake though I don't wish to be.

"Why?" you may ask.

I've had a lovely weekend watching my niece receive her master's degree in education here at William and Mary. The graduation service was late in the afternoon, so instead of driving home, we decided to spend the night here in Williamsburg, Virginia, a quaint little town. We rented a three-room suite, and currently my mom and brother-in-law are in opposing bedrooms snoring it out. The arrhythmic, apnea-induced cadence sounds somewhat like a cross between a flooded chainsaw trying to start and a couple of snarling pit bulls about to fight. Somehow, my sister and her son continue sleeping, but the racket is too great for my sensitive ears.

There's no telling how this sleep-deprived article is going to come out. Be prepared for some random and potentially bizarre thoughts.

One thing that has always puzzled me is this: Why did Satan fall?

I mean, I know he fell because he went against God and got thumped out of Heaven. Bible scholars often refer to Isaiah:

> How you are fallen from Heaven, O shining star, son of the morning. You have been thrown down to the earth, you who destroyed the nations of the world. For you said to yourself,

> "I will ascend to Heaven and set my throne above God's stars. I will preside on the mountain of the gods far away in the north. I will climb to the highest Heavens and be like the Most High." Instead, you will be brought down to the place of the dead, down to its lowest depths (Isa. 14:12–15 NLT).

But where's the logic here? Why would anyone go against God? Spock from Star Trek wouldn't do it. "It would be illogical, Captain."

Although I have no interest in interviewing Satan (I would prefer to stay as far away as possible from someone so evil), the whole scenario makes me want *somebody* to ask Herr Lucifer, "What the heck were you thinking?"

In the scripture above, you see a lot of "I"s. When it comes to sin and pride, the "I"s have it, but it would take an incredible amount of pride for one of the created to think that he could somehow overcome the Creator. Satan was (and still is) an incredibly powerful being; he was at the top of the food chain among the angelic host. How could someone so powerful and intelligent do something so foolish? It defies logic to be so close to God and witness all of His glory and yet become so blinded by personal pride that you try to overcome the very Being Who created you. It simply defies reason. Satan certainly didn't foretell the consequences of his future state.

So dear reader in your well-rested state, I now turn the question to you: "What are you thinking?" Are you in obedient service to God the Father, the Creator of the universe, or are you singing Lucifer's Medley, which starts with Frank Sinatra's "My Way" and concludes with AC/DC's "Highway to Hell"? Do you know which road you are on and where it will finally lead?

When I think about the Far-Left Liberals who have rebranded themselves as "Progressives," (I'll let the reader determine if this was a random or continuous thought transition) I wonder what they are progressing toward. The Second Habit in Stephen Covey's *The 7 Habits of Highly Effective People* is, "Begin with the end in mind." To put in best practices terms of defining a current and future state, what is the future state, what is the end goal envisioned? What's the objective? It often appears that the Progressive's goal is simply progress for progress' sake—just keep things moving then we'll figure out if it's the right direction. That makes as much sense as Speaker Nancy Pelosi's comment that we needed to pass the healthcare bill so we can find out what's in it. Somehow the suggestion of try reading the bill first logically comes to mind. Hmm. Maybe there's a trend here.

Even if you are unclear tactically where you are "progressing," it's relatively easy to determine strategically where you want to go and with whom. If you're doing it your way without God, then it's a secular progressive path. That leads to secular humanism where humans are the apex of priority. When you parse the humans out, you get some humans who are more equal than others—those with power and/or prestige above those with less power and prestige continuing down the scale to the weak, elderly, sick, or handicapped, and finally the unborn. We're already killing off the unborn in droves, and as mankind faces dwindling resources guess who'll be next? Just work your way backwards up the human food chain. It's love thy neighbor, but love them less if they are worth less.

That kind of progress is a helluva journey. It's not even progression; it's regression. This foolish path is the perfect embodiment of the concept contained in Proverbs 14:12: "There is a way that seems right to a man, but it leads to destruction." It leads to death. Some of our leaders think that their way seems right to them. Many of us at the back of the bus think that we're about to go over a cliff.

Any movement without Christ is moving backwards from where you want to go. It leads to destruction and death. When you reach the end, I don't think it matters whether you exalted yourself above God (Satan method) or removed God from the equation altogether (humanism method), as there is no partial credit for a less-wrong answer. Both are a total loss.

The only way to progress is with God through His Son Jesus Christ. It doesn't matter if you are a liberal, progressive, conservative, libertarian, or moderate. If you go with God, then you are going the right way. If not, it's going to be Hell.

41. The Shining

And God said, "Let there be

$$\nabla \cdot \mathbf{E} = \frac{\rho}{\varepsilon_0}$$

$$\nabla \cdot \mathbf{B} = 0$$

$$\nabla \times \mathbf{E} = -\frac{\partial \mathbf{B}}{\partial t}$$

$$\nabla \times \mathbf{B} = \mu_0 \mathbf{J} + \mu_0 \varepsilon_0 \frac{\partial \mathbf{E}}{\partial t}$$

And there was light" (Gen 1:3 NSB Nerdy Science Bible).[1]

Okay, a little geek humor—just thought you might get a charge out of it. The above are Maxwell's equations describing electromagnetic radiation or light. God is the omniscient Scientist. He is the original Author and Inventor of all creation. Human scientists can mathematically calculate how the laws work, but God created the laws in the first place. We should never make "light" of that fact.

We should however, be a light. Jesus said, "Let your light shine before men in such a way that they may see your good works, and glorify your Father who is in Heaven" (Matt. 5:16 NASB).

So let's break this divine directive down into its component parts. Our first requirement is to let our light shine. You can't have a light without a light source, and we can't shine without God. He spoke light into existence and He is the Source of all light—physical, intellectual, and spiritual.

This God-sourced light of ours is to shine before men or before all people. This means that we are to be an example to others. How? By having others see our good works. The best form of leadership is to lead by example. The best testimony is through your actions. Talk is cheap. When you walk the walk, your walk will talk the talk.

These works that we do are not just any works, but good works. As Jesus said, "Only God is truly good" (Luke 18:19b NLT). Therefore, these works must be those inspired by God to accomplish His will. Our role in this world is to submit to God and make ourselves available for His purpose to do His bidding. In a sense, we are all tools in God's toolkit, so when He reaches for us, we should not be stuck in our strap holder or hiding out down in the bottom of His bag. When we have surrendered our spirit to God's will, then we are ready for His use in accordance with His plan and we will produce good works.

One of the key parts of this verse is contained in the prepositional phrase, "in such a way." Our light is to shine in a particular manner. What is this manner or way? It is to be a blessing to others. The good works that we do should benefit our fellow man. We are to love one another as Christ loved us. The Greek word for this kind of love is *agape*. It is a selfless love—a love without judgment or a love provided without it being merited. We just give it. The King James Bible refers to this type of love as *charity*. Life is already tough, and we all have needs, so we should give of ourselves and help out one another through gentle words of encouragement and generous acts of kindness. Doing unto others as you would want done unto you is not complicated. It's not Maxwell's equations. Just do it.

A friend once loaned me a book to read. It was somewhat New Age so I wasn't too impressed overall, but the author coined a really neat word and it should be in the English language. We should strive to be *loveful.* We can be *thoughtful, mindful,* and *thankful*, but it would be best if we all were *loveful.* If the people of this world behaved in such a way, there would be so much light on this earth that we would not have an energy crisis.

Finally, what is the ultimate purpose for being a good example through our works of being loveful and a blessing to others? It is to give glory to God. He is our reason for being. He is our Creator and Lord. We give Him glory when we are used by Him for His purpose. Those who see our light will then recognize its source and give Him glory as well. It's a beautiful thing, and it is often contagious.

As you near the end of this book, we hope it has provided some light to you. Since there were several contributors to this book, we chose to publish it under the collective pen name, B.A. Brightlight.

Who is B.A. Brightlight? B.A. Brightlight is you. It's me. It is all who have accepted Christ as Savior. It is preachers, clergy, Bible scholars, and blue-collar faith-walkers. Our mission is to share our light through our love to others—to be a blessing to all we meet. It is not for our glory, but for the glory of the Source of all light. It is for the glory of God.

Now it's time for us to light it up. The whole world is in a crisis, and our nation has very serious challenges ahead. America has always been a light to others—the shining city on the hill. We citizens need to fix our electrical short and get US beaming again. Like most electrical applications, we need to be properly grounded—grounded in Christ.

Jesus is the light of the world, and we bask in His light. Through His in-dwelt Spirit in us, we should radiate His glow. That's one of our mission statements. So go out, crank up the wattage, serve and love others, and give them a Son-tan.

Be a bright light for the LORD.

42. Follow to the Letter

Dear Nephew:

How be-ist thee? I hope you are bear-and-snake free and are enjoying your time in the jungle. It's a cool opportunity that you have spending the summer camping and keeping hiking tourists safe up in the mountains, although I am sure that it gets a little lonesome. Not everyone is cut out to be a hermit.

So, since you have some time on your hands, I wanted to put together something for you to ponder as you pursue your career and your path in life. It gets very philosophical and theological, so it may take a few readings over time to absorb it all. It's more the theory than pragmatic practice, but hopefully it will be helpful in establishing some life rules or principles that can guide you with your decision making as you venture into the world.

What's the ultimate goal of a human life? Can it even be defined in universal terms, or is each life so unique that a particular path, goal, or methodology cannot be defined? We only have one life to live and it gets closer to ending with each passing second, so it behooves all of us, wherever we are in life, to plot the proper course and develop an optimum strategy to live life to the fullest to achieve the most benefit to ourselves.

One could state that every person desires success. This is true, but then we come back to the crossroads of "What is the definition of success?" The answer is almost as unique as each individual.

An appropriate metaphor for life is a journey, for life has many twists and turns, hills and valleys, smooth pavement, potholes, and an occasional "Bridge Out Ahead." Sometimes you go off-road and sometimes you even end up in a ditch, which is rarely an optimum place to be (that is spoken from personal experience.). If we use this metaphor and try to define the best way to travel, then perhaps we can develop a winning strategy for living a successful life.

Like any journey or trip, there are a few fundamental principles to successful travel: first, you have to know where you are going; next, you should pack the correct things and have the proper attitude during the trip; finally, there are certain "best practices" for your method of travel to maximize your enjoyment and fulfillment along the way. I call these the 5Ps of successful travel. Though the analogy of a physical trip is quite appropriate, this is referring to a spiritual journey, which is the most important journey in this life you will ever take.

The ultimate goal for every person should be to find fulfillment in their lives. People pursue many different paths and many different objectives to find this fulfillment. The famous French philosopher, Blaise Pascal once wrote: "All men seek happiness. This is without exception. Whatever different means they employ, they all tend to this end...they will never take the least step but to this object. This is the motive of every action, of every man, even those who hang themselves."

Whether it is happiness (a rather superficial pursuit) or joy, or fulfillment to use a more generic definition of being a success in all that you do, one certainly shouldn't get "hung up" in pursuing it, as that's definitely not a "Best Practice" solution!

But what should you pursue?

The world in which we live promotes a different value system than what Jesus taught. The world promotes wealth and fame as pinnacles of success. It's *Who Wants to Be a Millionaire?* or *American Idol* that captures the world's attention. The ultimate measure of success in the world would be someone who is so rich and powerful that they lend money to Bill Gates out of petty cash, they have warehouses full of trophies and personal awards, the paparazzi constantly track this person's movements to provide updates to an infatuated public, members of the opposite sex swoon at their appearance, and they are worshipped and idolized by all. That doesn't sound too shabby, huh?

Certainly worldly achievements and accomplishments are worthwhile and should be acknowledged. Wealth and fame are enablers to greater opportunities, but in the end they're irrelevant. Although people strongly desire and aspire to get on the celebrity "A" list, a better goal would be to get on the "G" list—God's list. The Book of Life is where you want your name to be. That's where it's happening—that's the best party in the whole universe, and the cool thing about it is that the fun lasts for all eternity. In a nutshell, this is *the Answer*.

In the consulting world, we talk about "best practices" or the right way to do things based on certain principles and experience. This concept applies to every activity in life. For a simple example, when you cross the street, "best practices" advises you to look both ways before crossing. The biblical word for best practices is wisdom, and wisdom comes from God. "The fear of the LORD is the beginning of wisdom: and knowledge of the Holy One is understanding" (Prov. 9:10 ERV). In any situation that you face, the answer to one question will help you choose the right path. The question is: "What is the wise thing to do?" If you apply these 5P principles, evaluate your situation, and then ask, "What is the wise thing to do?" then you will make sound choices and avoid tragedy and misstep along your journey.

So here goes. The 5Ps are: Priority, Perspective, Potential, Process, and Preparedness. These relate to a journey as: where are you going, what attitude to have, how do you make the most of this journey, the best way to travel, and how to "pack" for the trip.

Technically, you need to pack or be prepared before you start your journey. However, you must know where you are going and how you plan to get there before you know what to pack. You don't take your wool coat when you're headed to the beach, so we'll call the Preparedness P a prerequisite P.

Since you are an Eagle Scout, you understand the importance of being prepared, as this should be a fundamental part of your mindset in all that you do. The appropriate verse is Eph. 6:11 NIV: "Put on the full armor of God so that you can take your stand against the devil's schemes." Why? "For our struggle is not against flesh and blood, but against the rulers, against the authorities, against the powers of this dark world and against the spiritual forces of evil in the Heavenly realms" (Eph. 6:12 NIV).

It's a dangerous world out there—so, "Be clear-minded and alert. Your opponent, the devil, is prowling around like a roaring lion, looking for someone to devour" (1 Peter 5:8 NIV). The twelve points of the Scout Law are character traits. When you develop these traits, just as an athlete develops a skill such as hitting a baseball or throwing a football, they become tools in your "backpack" to use in appropriate situations. When you act with courtesy and have the attitude of kindness, helpfulness, and cheerfulness, then you interact with the world in a positive message of respect and love. When you are trustworthy, loyal, thrifty, and obedient, you demonstrate self-discipline to sound principles of integrity that should not be compromised. When you are reverent, you acknowledge through worship a Heavenly Father Who is Creator of all and entitled to all glory and honor.

Like going out on the camping trail, you also must be wearing the proper equipment. Using a sports analogy, a football player would be very unwise to run onto the field without his helmet (even if he has a very hard head, it wouldn't be sufficient), so too you should not venture forth without all your equipment. Paul talks about all of these in Ephesians 6, but I'll review just a few of them.

Put on the helmet of salvation. The helmet protects the head, and the head leads the body. This is the most critical of all, for without salvation, nothing else matters. If you were to accomplish the ultimate in worldly success as described previously, yet did not have salvation through Jesus Christ, then your life is a total loss, for what profit a person to gain the whole world and lose his soul (Mark 8:36).

The next piece of equipment is the breastplate of righteousness. The breastplate protects the heart, which is the dwelling place of the Holy Spirit and how God evaluates us—for God sees not as man sees; God looks at the heart (1 Samuel 16:7). Keeping your heart pure and righteous enables God to work His purpose through you. I'll talk more about this in a moment.

The last two pieces I want to discuss are the shield of faith and the sword of the Spirit. You are protected by your faith in the promises of God of sufficient grace and mercy and in His Son's death and resurrection. Through faith, you know that you will never be tested beyond your capacity to handle it (1 Cor. 10:13).

Last is the sword of the Spirit or the Word of God. The sword is both an offensive and defensive weapon. The Word of God is Truth. Remember, even the smallest truth can defeat the biggest lie and our adversary is the devil who is the father of lies (John 8:44), so resist him through your knowledge of the Word with the sword of Truth and he will flee from you (James 4:7). It is far more effective than bear repellent. (I hope you never have to use that.) This will prepare you well for your journey.

Now for the Travel Ps. The first P is Priority. As in any journey, you first must know where you are going or else you will wind up lost or wasting time going to worthless, dead-end places—as the mice in the maze would say, "No cheese down this tunnel." Life is a journey, and we should add that it is best traveled with a destination in mind. We need to know where we are going, not just in the ultimate sense—Heaven, although that applies—but to travel along according to God's purpose and destination for us.

The appropriate scripture is Matthew 6:33: "Seek God's Kingdom first, and His righteousness, and all these things [that you need] will be provided unto to you." Note that we should seek God's Kingdom *first.* We're not to seek it *sometime during life*, or put it in the Top Ten Must-Seek list: see the Grand Canyon, get married, make a million dollars, and seek God's Kingdom. No, we're to pursue it with the absolute highest priority. By seeking His Kingdom first, it is like putting on a pair of glasses from God behind our eyes so that we see the world from His "eternal" viewpoint. God's perspective and priority differ from the world's, so we must navigate through this life using His GPS system—call it God's Providence System. How important is this? It's top priority.

Jesus told several parables about the Kingdom of God, and a couple of quickies are found starting in Mathew 13:44 where the Kingdom of God (or Heaven) is like a treasure found in a field or like a pearl of great value. When you read these parables, note what the response of the person who discovered the treasure. He sold all that he had in order to obtain it. In other words, the Kingdom of God is worth all you got. So seek His Kingdom first and His righteousness (don't forget that, as we must also obey His commandments). What is God's promise in response? All that you need will be provided unto to you. It may not be all that you think you want, but it will be all that you need to have a successful journey.

The second P is Perspective. This is the proper attitude for our journey. The appropriate scripture is Proverbs 3:5–6 (NIV), "Trust in the Lord with all your heart and lean not on your own understanding.

In all your works and all your ways acknowledge Him and He will direct your path." Several things happen when we put our wholehearted trust in Him. First, it gives us confidence, for God will direct our path in the way we are to go. When you are walking along the path that God has set before you, you cannot improve upon your journey. Think about that for a moment. If you are in God's will following God's path for you, it's like an Old Milwaukee commercial—it doesn't get any better than this. Perhaps I shouldn't reference a beer commercial, but it fits so nicely. God has a plan for all of us, and we can never say, "You know God, that's not a bad way to go, but I've got a better idea." No way. God is perfect and His plan is perfect, and when we're in the center of the fairway of His plan, we are right where we need to be.

The second thing this gives us is peace of mind. If we're right where God wants us to be, then we don't have to worry about anything, as we have that peace of mind that passes all understanding (Phil. 4:7). This peace of mind enables you to be environmentally independent, which is a great frame of mind to have in dealing with the trials and tribulations of life. When you trust God with all your heart and He is directing your path, then you can walk with total confidence and enjoy the fruits of the Spirit of love, joy, peace, patience, kindness, etc. (Gal. 5:22) in any circumstance. You can be happy with a lot or little, be in a palace or prison and this peace of mind will enable you to not only endure whatever circumstance you are in (even alone atop a mountain being harassed by mosquitoes), but you can do so singing praises to God—see Acts 16:25.

The third P is Potential. Like the Army, we should in our journey through life be all that we can be. Our objective in life is to fulfill the purpose that God has planned for us. God guides us through our hearts. In Matthew, verse 5:8 states: "Blessed are the pure in heart for they shall see God." There is a direct correlation between our purity of heart and how God can direct us for His purpose. If our heart is only partially pure, He can use us only partially. A pure heart is not a perfect heart.

None of us have a perfect heart, for we all have sinned and fall short of the glory of God (Rom 3:23). A pure heart is simply an honest heart. God seeks a relationship with us and, as in all relationships; it requires honesty to operate effectively. We are to be open and honest with Him. We are to tell Him of all our thoughts, hopes, dreams, and fears with brutal honesty. He knows them already, but He wants us to relate to Him with complete integrity—to come to Him with a pure heart. We are to trust Him with our whole heart, and we are to be honest with Him—just a, "Here I am Lord, warts, imperfections and all." We can be angry, sad, hurt, or happy, whatever it is that we are experiencing, and it's okay with God. It's the integrity that counts.

This particular verse is from the Sermon on the Mount where Jesus makes several encouraging statements of blessing. When you read these, there are some that seem more beneficial, such as blessed are the merciful for they shall receive mercy, or blessed are the meek for they shall inherit the earth. Now, don't get me wrong. The pure in heart getting to see God is certainly cool, but I'd rather inherit the earth or get mercy or comfort. What's so great about seeing God? I mean technically, He's so Holy that you can't even look upon Him directly—it would vaporize you. Then I remembered something Jesus said. "Truly, I tell all of you with certainty, the Son can do nothing of His own accord, but only what He sees the Father doing, What the Father does, the Son does likewise" (John 5:19 ISV). By having a pure heart, we get to see God and see what the Father is doing. Like the popular saying, WWJD (What Would Jesus Do?), we can go and join in on the action.

When you combine these first four Ps, you have put on the full armor of God, which prepares you for every encounter. You have developed a sound travel plan that establishes your priority objective—seeking God's Kingdom and His righteousness first, which helps train your heart and mind to see life from His perspective, and He will provide for all your needs. You've established your path, by trusting in Him, which gives you both confidence and peace of mind in your journey. This maximizes your potential so that God can use all of you for His purpose and strengthens your confidence for you can "see" what the Father is doing. By knowing that you are right where the Father wants you, you can't be in a better place.

The reward you will have in your heart is beyond comprehension when you are aligned with Him. "Delight yourself in the Lord, and He will give you the desires of your heart" (Psalm 37:4 ESV). That's such a cool promise, you better keep your teeth brushed as you'll have a perpetual grin on your face.

The final P brings it all together. It is the Process by which you travel. There are many verses that describe this, but the verse I chose is John 15:12 (NASB): "This is My commandment, that you love one another, just as I have loved you." The Bible is a love story about the Creator and His constant pursuit of His beloved creation—mankind. When asked what the greatest commandment was, Jesus replied that you must love the Lord your God with all your heart, mind, body, soul, and strength (once again, it's all you got), and then He added that we shall love our neighbors as ourselves (Matt. 22:36–39). Upon these two commands rest all the laws, rules, and regulations of the whole Bible, and it has only one verb: love. We love God in the vertical—Him above us—and we love our neighbors in the horizontal as our peers. When put together, this forms the shape of the cross, where God so loved the world that He gave His only begotten Son that whoever believes in Him shall not perish, but have eternal life (John 3:16). It's an amazing love story.

In Paul's first letter to the Corinthians, he describes the importance of love as the vital ingredient in every action we take. The entire thirteenth chapter of 1 Corinthians is often referred to as the "love" chapter. In it, Paul states that even if we could talk to angels and we did it without love, it's just noise. If we knew everything about everything or had so much faith and power that we could move mountains but did it without love, it is worth nothing. If we were to sacrifice our life and it was not motivated by love, then it is a total waste. Love is the key motivation for all action. "Love is patient; love is kind and is not jealous; love does not brag and is not arrogant, does not act unbecomingly; it does not seek its own, is not provoked, does not take into account a wrong suffered, does not rejoice in unrighteousness, but rejoices with the truth; love bears all things, believes all things, hopes all things, endures all things. Love never fails" (1 Cor 13:4–8a NASB).

One final thought. You played sports enough so you know that in order to improve yourself, you have to work at it consistently. You can't just jump in a pool and be an expert swimmer or even play a clarinet well without practice. Spiritual growth and improvement requires the same level of dedication. You have to work at it in a consistent manner, and it takes time to develop. It's a lifelong process. As stated earlier, we all have just one life to live and we do not know how long we have. The clock is constantly ticking, and unfortunately there are no time outs nor is there a pause button that we can press. We are now closer to death than when you first started reading this, and that applies to everyone—the irony of life and death is that as soon as we are born, we are simultaneously both living and dying.

Referring once again to consulting best practices, when solving a problem you state what objective or where you want to be (Future State), evaluate where you are (Current State), and then determine the best way to get from where you are to where you want to be. In *The 7 Habits of Highly Successful People*, Stephen Covey states as the second habit to "begin with the end in mind." Knowing where you want to end up helps determine how to get there. Life's a journey best traveled with a destination in mind. Generically speaking, the objective in life is that everyone wants to be successful—it just depends on how each individual defines success.

In the final analysis, the only opinion that matters is God's and therefore we should be diligently focused on God's Kingdom both here on earth and in the life to come. At some point after this life on earth, we will all have to give an accounting for what we have done: "And inasmuch as it is appointed for men to die once and after this comes judgment" (Heb. 9:27 NASB). To succeed in this life is to stand before His Throne and hear God say to you, "Well done, good and faithful servant."

Actually, it may be even better than that. For those who have accepted Jesus Christ as their Lord and Savior, they have become adopted children of God and heirs to His Kingdom. Our Heavenly Father knows what is absolutely best for you, for your sister, for me, and for every person on the globe. He longs for a relationship with you and wants you to trust Him, not just for your needs, but to live a life that is full and fruitful. Our Heavenly Father wants to bless us, and He knows how. If given a choice between letting myself choose what is best for me or letting God choose what is best for me, who do you think would make the better decision? I think God would, and if you apply the same question to yourself, you will reach the same answer.

Paul tells us in the first couple of verses in chapter 12 of Romans that we are to offer ourselves as living sacrifices, to not be conformed to the world, but be transformed by the renewing of your mind in Christ Jesus. We must surrender our will and seek the will and direction from the Holy Spirit that dwells within us. I don't have all the answers here, as I have not even remotely mastered this part, because *surrendering, yielding,* and *sacrificing* are words that naturally do not appeal to me.

It's interesting in that as you grow in faith, you begin to notice the change in your prayer life. At first, we appeal to God as this cosmic genie—please give us our desires. Then as we mature, we begin to seek His Kingdom and think in terms of His Kingdom, and we pray for our Father to help us achieve goals that we think He wants us to achieve. This is a definite improvement, but it still has the concept of asking God, "What will you do for me?" The final stage is achieving that sense of surrender, trusting, and knowing that God has your best interests at heart. Then your prayers to the Father will be more like, "What will You do through me?" It's okay to ask God whatever you wish. He tells us to do so. Even Jesus asked before His crucifixion if there were a Plan B, for He wasn't too excited about Plan A. Yet, He concluded with, "Not as I will, but as Thou wilt." Similarly, as we grow in faith, we continue to ask for anything, but "be prepared" to accept His answer and have the obedience to follow through with it.

As God's adopted son, you should earnestly seek His will on earth as it is in Heaven. By doing so, you will receive His blessings, guidance, and grace. Then as one who has been truly faithful, you will be loved by God and He will look down upon you and say, "This is my son with whom I am well pleased." That, dear nephew, is true success and a journey that was traveled well.

Stay safe and lots of love,

Your Uncle

43. A Sweet Fragrance

Jack Wehmiller

Every now and then a person has the opportunity to watch real heroes at work. More often than not, it is an ordinary person doing an extraordinary thing. The "hero" almost always doesn't even think that they are doing anything special. As a matter of fact, they seldom want any recognition for what they have just done. They were doing what they perceived as necessary. There is something internal in them that says, "If not now, when? If not me, who?"

I have had the privilege of witnessing just such events. Allow me to tell about two of them that took place recently. In less than thirty seconds on January 12, more than 250,000 people were killed in the Port-au-Prince area of Haiti. Twice that many were left homeless, hurt, and forever changed. We all heard about it. We all saw it on the news. We all had a choice as to how to respond. These are stories about how some did in fact respond. This is about people who said, "I will be the one who goes."

Wave after wave of doctors, nurses, and other first responders flowed into Haiti almost immediately. They arrived along with supplies at the airport, which was only a short walking distance from the triage area and the operating tents. These tents were as large as what we would see when the circus came to town, and the activity around them was at a feverish pitch. The Marines were guarding all supplies and all of the relief workers. People had come from all over the world to do what they could.

The carnage was unimaginable. For every medical professional who came there were at least 100 new patients. This Caribbean island, known as Hispaniola with two countries divided only by a mountain range was the site of what we would learn to be mankind at its finest. It was as we have read about in Corinthians. The sweet fragrance of Christ was shared by those that came to help.

While there are language barriers and cultural differences between the Dominican Republic and Haiti, there was no differentiation in the fact that all of them were God's children and many of them were hurt very badly. The Dominican side of the island felt the tremors but experienced no real damage. No buildings down, no death, only a feeling that something was terribly wrong just a short distance over the mountains.

First came the reports of the quake. Then came the flood of ambulances and other emergency vehicles into towns such as Barahona close to the border and Santo Domingo (the capital a full ten hours of driving away), bringing people who were simply in the wrong place at the wrong time. The initial wave of help came directly to Port-au-Prince, but soon the Haitians that had left their country were receiving help throughout the Dominican Republic. Many had the chance to see the very best of what we as human beings have to offer. Medical teams of surgeons landing at the site of the disaster began to operate in fifteen-hour shifts with little rest before the next grueling stretch of amputations and repairing of shattered limbs. This was more than just adrenaline pumping through their veins. This was far more special than that. As I stated earlier, it was greater than ordinary people doing extraordinary things. It was extraordinary people doing amazing things.

It was humbling to watch—incredible to experience. As Paul Harvey would say, "But here is the rest of the story."

There were many who could not take vacation time and go immediately. Some were in school and couldn't leave that very day. In many cases they wanted to go, but just could not. In this situation in Haiti, the problem is so large that the need for help is going to last for decades. No one will be showing up too late to help.

Almost three months have passed, and Spring Break 2010 was upon us. As all of us know this is a big deal for young people in school. Fort Lauderdale and Panama City, Florida (better known to us in Georgia as the "Redneck Riviera"), are always on the hot list of places to go. I would venture to say that a poor community in the sugar cane fields just outside of Barahona, Dominican Republic, is not number three on the list of most college students looking for a relaxing destination in April. On my last trip to the island, I had been asked to assess medical and construction needs and report to several groups that wanted to go and do their part. One of those groups was a team of students from the Medical College of Augusta and a seasoned surgeon from Dalton, Georgia. It just so happened that the surgeon's daughter was one of those students. I gave them my report, and the trip was set for Easter weekend.

These students, I would come to find out, were very special. They brought military duffel bags full of medicine and supplies. They brought a wonderful enthusiasm. I am here to tell you that our future is brighter than what we have been told. There is a whole generation of humble, loving, and generous young people on the way to the fight. After a four-hour flight and a six-hour bus ride, we arrived at the Mission House in Barahona. The next day the twelve first- and second-year students and the doctor began their work with Haitian and Dominican families alike in what we know as Batey Seven. They were going to minister to both the physical and emotional needs of the "Invisible Poor." People they had never seen before and probably would never see again. And minister they did. I was not there for the entire trip, but I do know that on the first day, over 100 patients were seen.

Blood pressure problems were attended to, wounds were cared for, some minor surgery was done, and a tremendous amount of medicine was dispatched with love and caring. The best part came at the end of the day. We all walked around the village and played with the children. It was quite a crowd after going 100 yards or so. The kids were coming from every corner of the place. We had them riding on our backs; we were singing. It was glorious, just simply glorious. Twelve young people, a doctor, and myself, separated by a lot more than a plane flight and a bus ride—separated by more than lifestyle; but on that afternoon, we were all laughing in the same language. "The Twelve" were having the time of their lives, and I have no doubt that many of them will lead medical mission trips of their own in the near future.

I didn't witness what was done on the balance of this trip because I had meetings to attend back in the U.S. I do know that for good measure the team did some work on the construction of an orphanage that will house 105 youngsters when completed. We hear an awful lot about what is wrong with the world. There is an untold amount of murder and mayhem on the news every night. The political scene has many of us weary. We are treated to the sordid goings on in Hollywood each time we wait in line at the grocery store, but I want to remind us all that there still exists an innate goodness that keeps shining through when it is needed the most—an indomitable spirit that will not and cannot be suppressed. I saw it. I know that it exists.

I am reminded of a true story and think that I will close with it. There is a mountainside in the heart of France that has soil particularly conducive to growing lavender. The people seized on an economic possibility and built a factory further up the mountain. The men that worked in the factory each day had the sweet smell of lavender permeate their hair and clothing each and every day. The people in the village could not hear the whistle blow at the end of the work day, but as the workers arrived in the town each evening the sweet fragrance of the lavender went before them. The wives and children would actually recognize that their loved ones were home because of the fragrance in the air. There is a sign in a restaurant not far from where we live that says, "Everyone who walks through our doors makes us happy—some by arriving, some by leaving." Make the people you come in contact with happy because you arrived. Be a sweet fragrance.

44. The Greatest Threat... Spiritual Decay

This is an edited version of a research paper written by Lieutenant Colonel Robert Van Antwerp in 1992. Many of the warning signs forecasted then are coming to fruition now. Here is the paper's abstract:

This study examines the "real threat" to our national security—that we are no longer a "Nation Under God" and are no longer led by those who understand the spiritual dimension of leadership envisioned and demonstrated by our founding fathers. Our founding fathers knew and accepted their role as spiritual leaders and did their best to reflect that in the documents they produced. Most leaders today get caught up in the trap of "secular humanism" and neglect their responsibilities.

INTRODUCTION

The mighty eagle. As the storm approaches, lesser fowl head for cover, but the mighty eagle spreads his wings and with a great cry mounts on the powerful updrafts, soaring.

The eagle personifies America, soaring, free, strong, and powerful. As the eagle soared effortlessly in the midst of the storm, so God's people were able to rise on the wings of faith. Faith in God is embedded in American history and culture.

God has showered over 200 years of blessing upon America. As she acknowledged and obeyed God's plan, she was elevated from infancy to a place of world leadership marked by freedom, unprecedented wealth, and influence.

Then slowly—almost imperceptibly—she began to attribute her blessings not so much to God, but to man.[1] The lines of right and wrong have blurred. We are collectively wallowing in materialism, self-centeredness, and pride. "Courts that had once legislated against immorality began to grant freedom to every man to 'do that which was right in his own eyes' (Judges 17:6 and 21:5).[2] Has our nation's spiritual foundation crumbled? Have our leaders led us astray because they neglected the "spiritual dimension" of leadership? Will an army stand and fight for freedom, democracy, and the American way of life if there is no spiritual backbone?

My research has convinced me more than ever that we need to look back and rediscover the foundational truths behind the success of our nation and the Army. This study examines the "real threat" to our national security—that we are no longer a "nation under God" and are no longer led by those who understand the spiritual dimension of leadership envisioned and demonstrated by our founding fathers.

We talk often of threats to our national security, yet seldom discuss what I believe is the greatest threat—the spiritual decay of America. It affects the very fabric of our founding fathers' mosaic. The decay rots away the strengths of our society and the extension of that society, our armed forces. A central theme of military history is that the first key to understanding any armed force is to understand the society from which it comes. An armed force will be no stronger than the society it serves. A sick society can hardly produce healthy armed forces.[3] Our society is sick.

What was once a nation that was tolerant in the name of civil rights now openly condones and even flaunts perversion, immorality, and a host of attitudes that were once unthinkable. We have turned away from that which made America great—her faith in God coupled with spiritual leadership.

Little by little that faith has turned to relativism and secularism—not because it was forced upon us, but seemingly because we did not care. Whereas our founding fathers knew the importance of and accepted their role as spiritual leaders and did their best to reflect that in the documents they produced, most leaders today get caught up in the trap of "secular humanism" and neglect their spiritual responsibilities.

What about today's leadership? America's sons and daughters, the strength of our armed forces, will be the big losers unless spiritual leadership becomes an essential quality of our leaders at every level.

In their deliberations on July 29, 1775, Congress recognized the importance of meeting the spiritual needs of the soldiers of the Continental Army by allowing General George Washington to recruit chaplains.[4] General Washington said that faith in God undergirded the Continental Army during the anguish of Valley Forge and "sustained the Revolutionary Army when all else was gone."[5] We would probably be shocked today if Congress openly supported a "spiritual need" through legislation.

What then, is our spiritual responsibility to those we lead? National leaders cannot turn over their responsibilities of spiritual leadership to the "church" any more than military leaders cannot merely turn over the mantle of spiritual leadership to their chaplains. The strength of our nation and the effectiveness of our fighting forces depends on leaders who are spiritually responsible.

A SPIRITUAL FOUNDATION

Acting on prior instructions from the government at Williamsburg, on June 7, 1776, Delegate Richard Henry Lee of Virginia introduced a resolution into Congress calling for a declaration of independence. The Congress elected five men to prepare a document claiming nationhood and independence under international law. The five were John Adams, Benjamin Franklin, Roger Sherman, Robert Livingston, and Thomas Jefferson. After discussing what form the declaration would take, the committee appointed Jefferson to write the first draft. Congress approved the final draft and voted independence on July 2, 1776.

The Declaration bore intense resolve and reflected the soul and mind of America. It was written with an understanding that man's law cannot be arbitrary, without insulting the laws of nature and of nature's God. Truth can be known, sometimes so clearly as to be self-evident. God created men, and created them equal, endowing them with inalienable rights—rights that they could not give away and that no one could take from them.

Because God made men and gave them their rights, men create governments under God's law to protect those rights.[6]

America's founding fathers understood very well the principle that faith and freedom go together, and that one cannot survive long without the other. Daniel Webster, the great statesman and orator of the early days of the Republic, in a speech delivered on December 22, 1820, at Plymouth, Massachusetts, said:

> Finally, let us not forget the religious character of our origin. Our fathers were brought hither by their high veneration for the Christian religion. They journeyed by its light and labored in its hope. They sought to incorporate its principles with the elements of their society and to diffuse its influence through all their institutions, civil, political, or literary. Let us cherish these sentiments, and extend this influence still more widely, in the full conviction that that is the happiest society, which partakes, in the highest degree of the mild and peaceful spirit of Christianity.[7]

The signers of the Declaration of Independence stated:

> We therefore, the Representatives of the United States of America, in General Congress assembled, appealing to the Supreme Judge of the world for the rectitude of our intentions ... solemnly publish and declare that these united colonies are, and of right ought to be, free and independent states ... And for the support of this Declaration, with a firm reliance on the protection of Divine Providence, we mutually pledge to each other our lives, our fortunes and our sacred honor.[8]

Supreme Judge of the world, *the protection of Divine Providence*, and *sacred honor* were not empty phrases in the minds of the signers. Jefferson and the U.S. Congress were very much concerned that their cause was right with God.

The Declaration is also filled with John Locke's language, as well as his political ideas. His ideas are biblically based, as he was a devout Christian himself.[9] The Declaration has been called a revolutionary document. But its power came from its affirmation of truth long established.

A key idea in the Declaration of Independence is that of *self-evident truths*, truths so clear and obvious to the ordinary person that they require no proof. Ironically, the term *self-evident* is the one that most clearly shows the impact of Christianity on the Declaration.[10]

Thomas Jefferson believed it was sufficient to assert certain transcendent truths as self-evident. To him God's existence was manifest in creation. Jefferson was not here talking about the God of Islam, faith in whom laid the foundation for a different kind of social order altogether. He meant the God of the New Testament.[11]

Whether Jefferson was himself a Christian is in dispute, but he understood the society in which he lived and who his audience was. Jefferson was addressing Christians. "Therefore," warns the Apostle Paul in his letter to the Romans, "let every person be in subjection to the governing authorities. For there is no authority except from God" (Romans 13:1).

The writings of Paul in Romans 1 and 2 are the Biblical source for the Christian belief about self-evident truth. Paul uses two Greek phrases that correspond to the concept of being self-evident. In Romans 1:19 the words *phaneros en autois* mean *evident in themselves,* and in Romans 1:20 the words *tois poiemasin nooumena kathoratai* mean *by means of things that are made are understood, being clearly seen.*[12]

Paul uses both phrases in the context of what men know naturally by natural revelation, apart from the special revelation of Scripture. The apostle makes it clear that this is a general revelation through nature and through man's conscience. It is a revelation only of the first principles of truth and morality. This revelation comes upon men from God despite man's darkness and sinfulness. Its knowledge does not originate with man, but is a gracious endowment from man's Maker. All men know it naturally, both through conscience and through observing the natural order.[13]

The Declaration of Independence proclaims its rights theory with the words: "We hold these truths to be self-evident: that all men are created equal; that they are endowed, by their Creator, with certain inalienable rights; that among these are life, liberty, and the pursuit of happiness." These were rights ordained by God in the constitution of the universe. Whether or not the British acknowledged them was irrelevant because these rights were "self-evident"—clear and certain.[14]

Twentieth-century society has lost its foundation for an understanding of "rights." Most see rights as a matter of politics where the government can create and take them away. There is a great deal of talk about "human rights" and "civil rights" but the concept of "unalienable rights" is all but lost. This situation signals a crisis in modern political thought and threatens Western freedoms, since the concept of rights is "theory dependent."[15]

America was founded on "inalienable rights"—those that man may not unconditionally sell, trade, barter, or transfer without denying the image of God in himself.[16] *Inalienable* is another word for eternal, not subject to change under any circumstance. It implies that there are moral absolutes. Today, the rights theory of the founding fathers is routinely traced to secular tradition. Why should Americans care that the Biblical roots of our culture have been exchanged for a wholesale commitment to the prevailing secular philosophy? A major difference is that secular philosophy is based on notions of power, whereas Biblical politics is based on concepts of authority. In the secular view, nothing is ever impermissible because no lines are drawn that cannot be crossed.

In secular reasoning, whoever wields power can determine the content of laws, the extent, and even the existence of other people's freedoms. Biblical philosophy, on the other hand, admits to predetermined lines of authority, which the civil government is not permitted to cross. Personal rights and freedoms are God-given and inalienable; they do not exist merely for civil convenience or at the discretion of those who hold civil power. Our founding fathers clearly meant for all to maintain these God-given rights and freedoms unconditionally—not subject to conditional civil liberties—liberties granted by the government at its own convenience.

The American Revolution is not over. The ideals enshrined in the Declaration for which the founders fought and died—ideals of law, justice, equality, liberty, and inalienable rights, self-government—are barely understood in America today, much less in the rest of the world.[17] The American Revolution was more than a contest with England. It was and is a war to defend a vision about law, rights, justice, and the God-given dignity of man. The vision was inspired over time by the words of the Bible and the teachings of Christianity, but applies to all men everywhere regardless of their faith.[18]

Today, the Declaration's ideas are scoffed at, misrepresented, attacked, ridiculed, held in contempt, and ignored. The revolution is not over.

It is important for soldiers and leaders to know that the Declaration stands in the Judeo-Christian stream of political theory. Its legacy must be defended, since it is different both in degree and in kind from its secular counterpart, the French Revolution.[19] This has definite implications for those of us who lead those who pledge to fight and defend the Constitution of the United States against all enemies foreign and domestic.

Even if one does not accept the truth of the Christian faith, prudence argues for the promulgation of its moral code in every area of public life because history has demonstrated that Christian morality is indispensable to the preservation of a free society.[20]

Alexis de Tocqueville in the early part of the nineteenth century was commissioned by the French government to travel throughout the United States in order to discover the secret of the astounding success of this experiment in democracy. The French were mystified by the conditions of social tranquility and unparalleled freedom present in America. This is what Tocqueville reported:

> "I do not know whether all Americans have a sincere faith in their religion, for who can know the human heart—but I am certain that they hold it to be indispensable for the maintenance of republican institutions. This opinion is not peculiar to a class of citizens or to a party, but it belongs to the whole rank of society." America, Tocqueville added, is "the place where the Christian religion has kept the greatest power over men's souls; and nothing better demonstrates how useful and natural it is to man, since the country where it now has the widest sway is both the most enlightened and the freest."[21]

John Quincy Adams, America's sixth president, acknowledged that from the beginning Americans "connected in one indissoluble band the principles of civil government with the principles of Christianity."[22]

The colonists believed in a Higher Law—a definite thing that could be found in a particular place, namely the Bible, under whose commandments all would be equally subjected. Samuel Adams, the great revolutionary organizer, in his 1772 classic of political history The Rights of the Colonists, wrote: "The right of freedom being a gift of God Almighty,...the rights of the colonists as Christians...may be best understood by reading and carefully studying the institutes of the Great Law Giver...which are to be found clearly written and promulgated in the New Testament."[23]

Judges throughout English and American history have often handed down decisions with explicit references to the Ten Commandments, the Higher Law handed down by God to show us how to live with each other, how to order their moral lives and their community, and how to please Him. James Madison, known as the Father of the U.S. Constitution, put it this way: "We have staked the whole future of the American civilization, not upon the power of government, far from it. We have staked the future...upon the capacity of each and all of us to govern ourselves, to control ourselves, to sustain ourselves according to the Ten Commandments of God."[24]

In 1978, perhaps with some of this history in mind, the Kentucky Legislature required that the Ten Commandments be posted in the public schools along with the following statement: "The ten commandments secular application is the fundamental legal code of Western civilization and the common law of the United States."[25] But in 1980, the Supreme Court ruled that the posting of the Ten Commandments in Kentucky public schools was a violation of the First Amendment's clause forbidding the establishment of religion. This ruling essentially made it "unconstitutional" for public schools to teach the true origin of America's common law heritage, which undergirds the U.S. Constitution and which is specifically referred to in the Seventh Amendment.[26] Instead of protecting religion from the state, as our founding fathers had intended, we were protecting the state from religion. This 1980 ruling followed the already astounding 1962 decision banning all religious expression from the public schools. As a result of these rulings, many public schools have dropped Christmas programs and carols from their traditional Christmas celebrations. Our courts have misinterpreted what James Madison and Fisher Ames had in mind when they introduced the First Amendment. What was introduced to guarantee "the free exercise" of religion is being used to obliterate religion.

Every president, from George Washington to George Bush, has placed his hand on a Bible and asked for the protection of God upon taking the oath of office. Both Houses of Congress open each daily session with prayer.[27] "In God We Trust" is forever present on our currency. Witnesses in court are expected to swear on the Bible that they will "tell the whole truth and nothing but the truth, so help me God." Each day's session of the Supreme Court is opened with, "God save the United States and the Honorable Court." By ruling of the Supreme Court, the Ten Commandments cannot appear in our schools but appear on the wall above the head of the Chief Justice in the Supreme Court.

Man has a religious nature that he can never escape. The atheists, like Madalyn Murray O'Hare and Bertrand Russell, are as religious as Mother Teresa, John Wesley, and Martin Luther.[28] The atheist believes wholeheartedly that God does not exist and that there is no life after death. The theist, on the other hand, believes that God does exist and that one's choices here on earth have a bearing on one's eternal destiny. Most soldiers, when confronted with their own mortality, are theists.

Agnosticism is no less of a faith than Christianity or atheism. The agnostic does not know if God exists, but believes that if God exists, it makes no difference in his life. America has become politically and culturally agnostic, and the Christian faith in the minds of many has come to represent intolerance. The notion of moral absolutes sounds authoritarian and dogmatic even to some Christians.[29] We are offered an alternative in "pluralistic agnosticism," connoting a non-confrontational, live-and-let-live lifestyle. An example is the Supreme Court's abortion ruling, which overturned laws in all fifty states and condemned millions of unborn babies to slaughter with a stroke of the pen. The majority opinion states explicitly that "religious belief can have no bearing on how we determine when human life begins." Even William O. Douglas, one of the most liberal Supreme Court justices in history, admitted that "we are a religious people whose institutions presuppose a supreme being."[30] Agnostic pluralism releases man from the constraints placed on him by God and raises man up as the measure of all things.

The real danger is that we are shifting away from the God of Scripture, immutable and unchanging, toward the god of human convenience. Formally, this philosophy is not called pluralism, but secular humanism—the view that man is the sole judge of the world, including morality, the shape of society, and the value of the individual.[31] Those who take stands on Christian doctrines condemning sex outside of marriage, abortion, and homosexuality are quickly labeled and become victims of the American Civil Liberties Union, Planned Parenthood, People for the American Way, abortion rights groups, and others.

THE GROWING THREAT—A CRUMBLING HOUSE

Until about thirty years ago, the name "America" would evoke a feeling of pride, gratitude, and hope. America's moral and fiscal currency was the soundest in the world. We were the Free World's policeman; an encouraging older brother to those young nations struggling to achieve democracy and the hope of all peoples still in bondage.[32] At home we were confident that we were making the world a better place in which to live.

There had been a gradual, sustained improvement that most men could trace in their own lifetimes and the future looked promising. We were technologically superior and breakthroughs were a daily happening. Medically, we were on the verge of conquering every disease known to man.[33] In a word, *optimism* summed up America.

All of a sudden, everything went out of balance. Our military ventures ceased to go according to plan. We were actually in danger of losing. A president who personified the American Dream was assassinated. Young people began to lash out at authority and escape into the "mindless self-destruction of drug abuse."[34] Nations we had helped turned against us with hatred and our foreign policy devolved into one of reaction.

On the home front, our economy became erratic and became a destabilizing factor among the people. Suddenly our children were two years behind the averages of a decade before by college entrance standards. Mathematics and English aptitudes were plummeting. Industry gave way to services and a greater percentage of the population was on welfare than ever before. Our optimism was turning to despair. In a few short years, the public sector ballooned so that it now consumes over one-third of the entire U.S. economy—and most of this has occurred since the ban on prayer in public schools in 1962.[35]

But perhaps the most telling indicator of our condition was the extent of our moral decay. We scrambled to accommodate sexual promiscuity through permissive sex education, more effective and available birth control, and legalized abortion. The family unit was disintegrating, heretofore the thread that kept American fabric together. The divorce rate approached one failed marriage in two, child abuse soared, and parents abdicated their traditional roles of leadership.[36]

Alexis de Tocqueville foresaw the likely consequences of permitting the erosion of America's moral foundations and predicted that if this occurred, we would see the rise of a new form of despotism, unique to democratic societies:

> Over its people will stand an immense, protective power, which is alone responsible for securing their enjoyment and watching over their fate...it gladly works for their happiness but wants to be the sole agent and judge of it. It provides for their security, foresees

> and supplies their necessities, facilitates their pleasures, manages their principal concerns, directs their industry, makes rules for their testaments, and divides their inheritances....Thus, it daily makes the exercise of free choice less useful and more rare, restricts the activity of free will within a more narrow compass, and little by little robs each citizen of the proper use of his own faculties.[37]

We hit the depths of despair when our President, the symbol of all that was right and decent in America, was caught lying to the people and manipulating our trust.

What happened to the American Dream? The truth is that the Dream is turning into a nightmare. Our founding fathers gave us the answer. They knew this nation was founded by God with a special calling. The people who first came here knew that they were being led here by the Lord Jesus Christ, to found a nation where men, women, and children were to live in obedience to Him. This was truly to be "One Nation Under God."

The reason, I believe, that we Americans are in such trouble today is that we have forgotten, rejected, and become cynical about being "Under God." We, as a people, have thrown away our Christian heritage.

The free world is threatened now, not because of lack of resources, but from a spiritual and moral void, which is always accompanied by a corrosion of the will. With religious expression now outlawed from large portions of American public life—in the name of a very distorted civil-libertarian creed—can it be long before America goes the way of Greece and Rome of old? Tocqueville had this to say of those who attack faith in God in the name of pluralism:

> When such men as these attack religious beliefs, they obey the dictates of their passions, not their interests. Religion is much more needed in the republic they advocate than in the monarchy

> they attack, and in democratic republics most of all. How could society escape destruction if, when political ties are relaxed, moral ties are not tightened?[38]

Asked Tocqueville: "What will happen to a people master of itself if it is not subject to God?"

History is strewn with the remains of nations, once great, who let the decay from within bring them to ruin. Historians record in the Rise and Fall of the Roman Empire how the Empire rose to greatness. Prosperity, excellence in culture and architecture, discoveries in medicine were but a few of the reasons its citizens assumed that the Empire would be around for centuries to come. Greek civilization rose to its "Golden Age" and gave the world its first historical attempt at democracy. Soon corruption set in and infiltrated every aspect of Greek life—even religion. In time Greece fell, and with it democracy, because it lacked the moral fiber and spiritual leadership to undergird it.

Other great civilizations have come and gone as corruption took hold. Today they are merely ghosts of the past with little to show for their great achievements and victories.

Does the same black shadow already loom over America? Civilizations do not just die. Their leaders and people are first deceived; then they are destroyed by God. Eph. 5:6 says, "Let no man deceive you with vain words: for because of these things (immorality, covetousness, worship of false gods, etc.) cometh the wrath of God upon the children of disobedience." Do we already believe "the lie" that was first given to Eve in the garden of Eden: "...ye shall be as gods, knowing (deciding for yourselves) good and evil" (Gen. 3:5)?

When a nation listens to *the lie,* it dethrones God and defies man's achievements. It exalts human reason as supreme. It trusts education and science to solve its problems. It believes that man is evolving into perfection. It replaces God's moral standards with situational ethics.

It promotes sensual pleasure and instant gratification. It strives for a world utopia of prosperity and peace. It makes the State the sovereign dictator over everyone.[39]

Rome believed the lie. Man became the measure of all things. The human body was idolized. Only the strong survived. "Rome was quite tolerant of all religions except Christianity. Christianity was banned and Christians were persecuted, burned, and thrown to the lions."[40] Why? Because the very nature of Christianity is contrary to the lie that man and the human mind are supreme, the basis of every other religion.

America is in danger, and the greatest threat to our national security is from within. We may feel invincible and destined to lead the world for decades to come, but already we are exhibiting characteristics of civilizations that have disintegrated and disappeared.

Fortunately, many are alert to the impending danger. They are calling America to wake up and resume our rightful position as a "Nation under God." The survival of our nation and our Army depends on it.

Spiritual strength begins with individual faith. Our hope lies in the promise that God made to Israel when she was an infant nation realizing that she would drift towards believing "the lie." "If my people which are called by my name will humble themselves and pray and seek My face and turn from their wicked ways, then I will hear from Heaven and will forgive their sin and heal their land" (2 Chron. 7:14).

On April 30, 1863, President Abraham Lincoln called for a National Day of Fasting, Humiliation, and Prayer, stating:

> We have been the recipients of the choicest bounties of Heaven. We have been preserved, these many years, in peace and prosperity. We have grown in numbers, wealth and power, as no other nation has ever grown. But we have forgotten God. We have forgotten the gracious hand, which preserved us in peace, and multiplied and enriched and strengthened us; and we have vainly imagined, in the

> deceitfulness of our hearts, that all these blessings were produced by some superior wisdom and virtue of our own. Intoxicated with unbroken success, we have become too self-sufficient to feel the necessity of redeeming and preserving grace, too proud to pray to the God that made us. It behooves us, then to humble ourselves before the offended Power, to confess our national sins, and to pray for clemency and forgiveness.

President Lincoln clearly understood that the nation needed to turn back to God, to commit to Him, and to begin rebuilding the spiritual foundations that had been crumbling. What Lincoln understood in 1863 is even more clearly seen today—the growing threat to America—the house crumbles from within.

Before his death, Thomas Jefferson also saw the inevitable result of continuing in our present direction. He said, "Indeed, I tremble for my country when I reflect that God is just, and that His justice cannot sleep forever."[41] The spiritual strength of our nation will determine the strength of our armed forces.

Personal faith and spiritual strength are keys to a soldier's ability to function under combat stress. Just as we cannot afford to neglect the spiritual condition of our nation we must realize that the success of our Army on any future battlefield will to a great extent depend on the spiritual condition of our soldiers.

SOLDIERING—THE SPIRITUAL DIMENSION

Modern historians have come to realize that the first key to understanding any armed force is to realize that it is an extension of the society that created it. A corollary is that an armed force is likely to be no stronger than the society it serves. With the erosion of a nation's religious life, we inevitably find a dissipation of the will. Americans have lost sight of the fact that a price must be paid for freedom. The preservation of liberty sometimes involves personal sacrifice. Americans in the past have believed that there are certain values more precious that life itself, and one of those is freedom.

Ancient Greece ultimately collapsed because the Greek philosophy never provided individuals a rationale for making sacrifices in defense of principle. The perpetuation of the state, or even of the society, was not, in the final analysis, reason enough to lay down one's life. The average Athenian felt a sense of isolation, rootlessness, and that he was living a life without purpose. Athenian soldiers' will to fight and defend the state deteriorated with the will of the people. Ancient Greece imploded into a spiritual abyss before it was defeated by the Macedonians in the fourth century B.C.

Perceptive leaders recognize the significance of faith and spiritual strength to sustain soldiers in battle. Soldiers with combat experience have confirmed that judgment. General George C. Marshall said:

> I look upon the spiritual life of the soldier as even more important than his physical equipment. ... The soldier's heart, the soldier's spirit, the soldier's soul are everything. Unless the soldier's soul sustains him, he cannot be relied upon and will fail himself and his country in the end. It's morale—and I mean spiritual morale—which wins victory in the ultimate, and that type of morale can only come out of the religious nature of the soldier who knows God and who has the spirit of religious fervor in his soul. I count heavily on that type of man and that kind of Army. [42]

Why do American soldiers fight? Are we equipping them properly? In considering these questions, Samuel Stouffer in The American Soldier: Combat and Its Aftermath, investigated the motivational factors that increased the soldier's resources for enduring combat stress. [43] As a result of an extensive survey, he found that faith in God and prayer were crucial to enduring combat stress for the majority of soldiers:

> The only other item approaching prayer in the proportion of men who said it helped them a lot was thinking that 'you couldn't let the other men down'—touching on potent forces of group solidarity and loyalty—but in both theaters (European and Pacific) more of the men, regardless of educational level or of whether they were privates or noncoms, said that prayer was helpful.[44]

Stouffer noted that men with combat experience were "more likely than men who did not see combat to agree that their Army experiences had increased their faith in God."[45] He found that 79 percent of WWII combat veterans reported increased faith in God.

Military historians and theorists have long recognized the influence of personal faith and spiritual strength on the soldier's ability to function under combat stress. Success on any future battlefield will depend upon the spiritual condition of our soldiers.

In describing the actions of his unit during an ambush in Vietnam, an American soldier said, "We all asked the help of the Lord that night."[46]

My experience during seven months in Saudi Arabia for Desert Shield/Desert Storm is that even the hardest, most irreligious appearing soldiers find time to pray when confronted with death and their own mortality.

When the Second Continental Congress gathered on May 10, 1775, under the leadership of John Hancock, they were looking for the one man who could lead them to victory over a mother country who was determined to suppress the "revolt." They needed someone who could transform a part-time militia of farmers, merchants, and preachers into a disciplined army. John Adams proposed George Washington as the obvious choice. On June 15, he was unanimously selected to lead America into war. He said he would accept the command only on the condition that Congress appoint and fund chaplains for his troops, which Congress promptly did.[47]

Washington was a committed and a believing Christian who preferred a more private religious life marked by a living faith.[48] Historians have avoided discussing Washington's religious life yet it can be seen that he was a devout Christian by looking at his private prayer book written in his own handwriting. The very first entry in the Daily Sacrifice reads as follows:

> Almighty God, and most merciful Father, who didst command the children of Israel to offer a daily sacrifice to Thee, that thereby they might glorify and praise Thee for Thy protection both night and day...I beseech Thee, my sins, remove them from Thy presence, as far as the east is from the west, and accept of me for the merits of Thy Son Jesus Christ....Let my heart, therefore, gracious God, be so affected with the glory and majesty of (Thine honor) that I may not do mine own works, but wait on Thee....As Thou wouldst hear me calling upon Thee in my prayers, so give me grace to hear Thee calling on me in Thy word, that it may be wisdom, righteousness, reconciliation and peace to the saving of my soul in the day of the Lord Jesus.

His second entry, written at the close of the day reflects acknowledgement of who God is:

> O most glorious God, in Jesus Christ...I acknowledge and confess my faults, in the weak and imperfect performance of the duties of this day. I have called on Thee for pardon and forgiveness of sins, but so coldly and carelessly that my prayers are become my sin and stand in need of pardon. I have heard Thy holy word, but with such deadness of spirit that I have been an unprofitable and forgetful hearer....Let me live according to those holy rules which Thou hast this day prescribed in Thy holy word....Direct me to the true object, Jesus Christ the way, the truth and the life. Bless, O Lord, all the people of this land.[49]

General Washington clearly understood the spiritual dimension of soldiering as it applied to his own life and the life of those he was to lead. It was no mistake he was chosen to lead the Continental Army. That Army has become the standard, the spiritual yardstick that others are measured against.

Major General Barry R. McCaffrey, in an address to the Army War College on August 14, 1991, stated, "The Desert Storm Army was made up of the most religious soldiers since [Washington's] army of Northern Virginia." Yet my experience in Desert Storm elicits a different observation. The Desert Storm Army that I observed had only a very small percentage of soldiers who brought a personal faith with them to the desert. What did surface after deployment was a greater sensitivity to spiritual things among soldiers. Many of those who struggled with life in the desert, priorities, loneliness, family separations, and their own mortality sought answers to life's tough questions. When confronted with their own lack of control over their destiny and circumstances (the basis for "secular humanism") many turned to God. Some found new life in Jesus Christ as He became the answer to the tough questions. This confirmed the old adage that "there are no foxhole atheists." Very few leaders had considered the spiritual dimension of soldiering and the role of faith in sustaining the soldier prior to deployment. Consequently, both leaders and soldiers were not equipped. The months before combat did provide some time to "train" on spiritual things but we fell far short because of the years of neglect. Spiritually, today's Army falls far short of the Continental Army. The soldier, on the other hand, has a hunger for spiritual things that is accentuated when in crisis. Washington put a premium on the spiritual training and equipping of his soldiers because he understood the possible hardships his army was to undergo and the sustaining nature of faith.

In 1985, speaking at Fort Monmouth, New Jersey, General John W. Vessey, Jr., said, "The spiritual health of the Armed Forces is as important as the physical health of its members or the condition of its equipment."[50] General Vessey's statement was rooted in experience and reflected years of observing soldiers in and out of combat. He demonstrates a keen awareness of the need for spiritual training and leadership to insure spiritual health.

Clausewitz is widely acclaimed for having "broken with the sterile material-oriented theories of the seventeenth and eighteenth centuries and for having brought the human, moral, and psychological factor back into the theory of war."[51] In recent times, more and more leaders have become aware that faith and spiritual wellbeing are important in the lives of soldiers and their families.

The importance of faith in a combat environment is well documented. There are striking instances where faith and the spirit that resulted enabled a small number of soldiers to have a far greater impact than anyone could imagine. The defense of Little Round Top at the battle of Gettysburg was just such an instance. The 20th Maine—350 strong, commanded by Col. Joshua Chamberlain, minister of the gospel of Jesus Christ and college professor—held their defensive position against overwhelming odds. The attackers remarked that the defenders had no fear, as if they already knew the outcome.[52]

Faith can supply hope because we know we are not alone and because God knows the outcome. Jesus Christ tells us that He will never leave us or forsake us. It is our hope in His promises and in Him that enables us to stand firm in the face of overwhelming odds. Hope is needed to dispel the fear that can immobilize even the fiercest warrior. Whereas fear can make one visualize the worst in everything, faith gives us hope for the best and a peace about the future.

Faith links us to values worth fighting for, sacrificing for, dying for. During a crisis we tend to more closely examine our lives and that which is important. People who experience tragedy in their lives will tell you that it reorders their priorities.

Leaders must be as capable of evaluating the moral and spiritual fitness of the soldiers in their units as they are of evaluating physical fitness or technical competence.

SPIRITUAL LEADERSHIP

When Washington took command of the Continental Army at Cambridge on July 2, he immediately sent out an order forbidding "profane swearing, cursing and drunkenness. And in like manner," the order stated, "he [Washington] requires and expects of all officers and soldiers, not engaged in actual duty, a punctual attendance of Divine services, to implore the blessing of Heaven upon the means used for our safety and defense."[53] He also added that a national day of fasting on July 20 would be "religiously observed by the forces under his command exactly in the manner directed by the Continental Congress." Moreover, said Washington's order, "it is expected that all those who go to worship do take their arms, ammunition and accoutrements, and are prepared for immediate action if called upon."[54]

General Washington was a man of deep personal faith and clearly understood the spiritual dimension of soldiering. He believed that "there would not have been a Revolutionary victory and the birth of a new nation without God's intervention and blessing."[55] Moreover, his soldiers understood and accepted his spiritual leadership. That, combined with his presence and constant example, gave them strength to endure incredible hardships and defeat a better equipped enemy. The Continental Army was clearly a reflection of the society, which it served. The society was God fearing, upright, enduring, and understood the need to be under authority—first of God and then of those appointed over them.

Even though the Army has provided chaplains for our units for over 200 years, very little has been said about the spiritual role of the leader. While our literature is replete with material focusing on competencies and characteristics essential for leaders, spiritual faith and the spiritual requirements of our leaders are seldom addressed. Leaders of our nation and our nation's soldiers need to know the importance of spiritual leadership, a role they cannot abdicate. Even Clausewitz recognized the importance of intellectual, moral, and spiritual strength in superior nations and armed forces. He stated that all military action is "intertwined with geistige," intellectual and spiritual forces and effects.[56] He was concerned that military theory not ignore "these subjective forces which are precisely most decisive" when studying warfare.[57]

The great task ahead must be to return to first principles, principles upon which America's founders were in overwhelming agreement. They were firmly convinced that liberty was essential to happiness and prosperity in this world; that constitutional government was essential to liberty; that the preservation of both was contingent on Christian morality that could not long stand without firm faith in Christ. As Tocqueville wrote: "Liberty regards religion as its companion in all its battles and triumphs, as the cradle of its infancy and the divine source of its claims."

FM 22-100 states that, "What you are (your beliefs, values, ethics, and character) is the most important part of your leadership."[58]

In his book entitled *Leadership*, James MacGregor Burns states, "Moral leadership concerns him the most...moral leadership is not mere preaching, or the uttering of pieties, or the insistence on social conformity...but emerges from, and always returns to the fundamental wants and needs, aspirations, and values of the followers...the kind of leadership that can produce social change that will satisfy follower's authentic needs."[59]

In his book, *The Closing of the American Mind,* Allan Bloom looks at American higher education and concludes that man longs for something we have lost—the kind of substance that gave meaning to the Declaration of Independence in which men pledged "their lives, their fortunes, and their sacred honor."[60] Bloom points out that in years past students arrived at the University already possessing an educational heritage rooted in the Bible, the family, and the American political tradition centered on the Declaration of Independence—"The Bible was the common culture, one that united the simple and the sophisticated, rich and poor, young and old."[61]

General of the Army Omar Bradley made these comments after WWII, "With the monstrous weapons man already has, humanity is in danger of being trapped in this world by its moral adolescents. Our knowledge of science has clearly outstripped our capacity to control it. We have many men of science; too few men of God. We have grasped the mystery of the atom and rejected the Sermon on the Mount. Man is stumbling blindly through a spiritual darkness while toying with the precarious secrets of life and death. The world has achieved brilliance without wisdom, power without conscience. Ours is a world of nuclear giants and ethical infants. We know more about war than we know about peace, more about killing than we know about living. This is our twentieth-century's claim to distinction and to progress."[62]

We are in danger as a nation and an army. As we move toward secular humanism and relativism there is a frightening possibility that we will lose God's blessing, the Spirit of America, and our fighting spirit as soldiers. The soldier is spiritually hungry. Chaplain (Col) David Peterson, Central Command Staff Chaplain for Desert Shield/Desert Storm said that commanders and senior NCOs had underestimated the spiritual interests and needs of their soldiers in the desert.[63] Leaders at every level sensed a personal requirement to actively support their soldiers spiritually and meet their spiritual needs. Many leaders found themselves ill equipped to meet this need because of their lack of personal faith and spiritual training. They were good at military training and equipping the soldiers tactically but rarely considered the spiritual climate of their unit to be an important part of the command climate. In many units the term "combat ready" not only meant training hardened soldiers but a "hardness" evidenced by hard talk, hard drinking, and hard—immoral—living. In Southwest Asia, commanders discovered a new dimension to combat readiness—faith. They discovered that the "moral/spiritual fiber of the soldier is an absolutely, critically important part of being ready for the ultimate mission."[64]

Leaders cannot ignore the soldier's need for spiritual training and the need to see model spiritual leaders any more than they can ignore tough, demanding field training, leadership development and leadership by example. Spiritual leadership is critical to our Nation and our Army. This type of leadership is provided by those who have a strong personal faith, a leadership style based on Biblical principles, and have developed the proper spiritual climate in their units and organizations. When leaders put a premium on the value of being "Under God" then there is hope. We dare not take anything for granted.

A STRONG PERSONAL FAITH

Spiritual leadership can be exercised only by Spirit-filled men and women. One must be personally "Under God" before he can hope to bring his unit "Under God." However brilliant a man may be intellectually, however capable an administrator, without a personal relationship with Jesus Christ, he is incapable of giving truly spiritual leadership. "Reduced to its simplest terms, to be filled with the Spirit means that, through voluntary surrender and in response to appropriating faith, the human personality is filled, mastered, controlled by the Holy Spirit."[65] Under the Spirit's control, natural gifts of leadership are refined and sanctified (used God's way).

The reason personal faith is so important is that it provides the foundation for who we are and how we lead. It is impossible to understand God's plan without it. With faith goes accountability and conformance. Ultimately we are accountable to God for our actions. Our concern should be whether or not our actions accentuate that which is against

God. We are to be conformed to the image of His Son, Jesus Christ. From Him we see the master principle for leadership—servanthood. The contrast between the world's idea of leadership and that of Christ is brought into sharp focus in Mark 10:42–43: "You know that those who are recognized as rulers of the Gentiles lord it over them; and their great men exercise authority over them. But it is not so among you. But whoever wishes to be first among you shall be slave of all."

It is a general principle that we can lead and influence others only so far as we ourselves have gone. "The person most likely to be successful is one who leads not by merely pointing the way but by having trodden it himself."[66] The same is true when considering the spiritual dimension of leadership. We are leaders to the extent that others are inspired to follow us. Only by believing in the need for a personal faith ourselves will we be able to encourage those we lead to develop their personal faith.

A LEADERSHIP STYLE BASED ON BIBLICAL PRINCIPLES

"Leadership is influence, the ability of one person to influence others. One can lead only to the extent that he can influence them to follow his lead."[67] Spiritual leadership is a blending of natural and spiritual qualities. Even the natural qualities are God-given and can only reach their highest effectiveness when employed in His service—"Under God."

In his book, *Spiritual Leadership*, J. Oswald Sanders compares some of the dominant characteristics of natural and spiritual leadership. While they have many points of similarity, they also have many points of dissimilarity.

[68]**Natural**	**Spiritual**
Self-confident	Confident in God
Knows men	Also knows God
Makes own decisions	Seeks to find God's will
Ambitious	Self-effacing

Originates own methods	Follows God's methods
Enjoys commanding others	Delights to obey God
Independent	God-dependent

Are Biblical qualities of leadership compatible with leading soldiers? The answer is a resounding "Yes." Judge for yourself as you compare the following, essential, Biblical leadership qualities with what you would desire in your subordinate leaders.

Great leaders, both natural and spiritual, have always been great encouragers. In these days of discouragement and disillusionment, this trait is even more crucial. We all should lean toward encouragement-slanted leadership. Hebrews 10:25 exhorts us: "Let us encourage one another, and all the more, as you see the day drawing near."

Leaders must be disciplined. They are able to lead because they have conquered themselves. Many are unable to lead because they have never learned to follow. They have never learned to be accountable and practice good followership. Generally others are willing to accept the discipline and follow a strongly disciplined leader more readily and cooperatively. He has set an example to be copied and conformed to. Leaders under the authority of God understand followership and discipline.

Men of faith have vision, for faith is vision. Vision includes foresight and insight and includes both optimism and hope. "No pessimist ever made a great leader."[69] This vision sees through the eyes of an optimist who sees an opportunity in every difficulty and sees God's hand working to refine, restructure and redirect. He can see good coming from bad because his trust in the only one who sees the future—God.

Decisive action characterizes a spirit-led leader. When in the will of God, one can press on, regardless of the consequences. The vision that comes through faith demands decisive action. We must do something about what we have seen and heard. Procrastination and vacillation can be fatal to good leadership.

In reply to a question, a prominent business man said, "If I had to name the one most important quality of a top manager, I would say, personal integrity—sincere in promise, faithful in discharge of duty, upright in finances, loyal in service, honest in speech."[70] The quality of personal integrity would probably be on everyone's list—maybe at the top. Ultimately our integrity is based on "to whom we are responsible." If one is accountable to God then they must be reminded that there is no time or place that escapes His scrutiny. Crucial to this quality is one's ability to honestly admit mistakes and shortcomings.

One quality that many of our leaders lack is courage. It takes courage to take the harder right rather than the easier wrong. It takes courage to follow your convictions in light of severe peer pressure and opposition. "The courage of a leader is demonstrated in his being willing to face unpleasant and even devastating facts and conditions with equanimity and then acting with firmness in the light of them, even though it means incurring personal unpopularity."[71] Faith enables us to have courage in our convictions and to realize that God's ways are worth pursuing in the face of adversity.

Webster's Dictionary defines our next quality, wisdom, as "the faculty of making the use of knowledge, a combination of discernment, judgment, sagacity, and similar powers." In Scripture, wisdom refers to right judgment concerning spiritual and moral truth. Wisdom takes into account people's experiences, weaknesses, and strengths. It involves the knowledge of God with insight into man's heart. It is the right application of knowledge in situations where the solution is not obvious. With wisdom goes understanding.

The final quality to be discussed is peace. Most "leadership lists" would not include this quality although it is essential to effective, spiritual leadership. It takes peace to be a good leader. Of the years of recorded civilization, very few have been without war. This is true with individuals too; how few people live a life that is calm and free from anxiety. The Jewish word *shalom* means peace—"keeping your mind firmly fixed on God" and adjusting your life accordingly. Peace comes from trust, which comes from faith. Totally trusting God gives peace. The leader that possesses this quality will be more tolerant, calm, relaxed, patient, less concerned about himself—at peace.

SPIRITUAL CLIMATE

Command climate provides the environment in which the job gets done. A major sub-climate and emphasis area within the command climate must be spiritual climate. To what degree is it acceptable to be a person of faith within this unit? Is it encouraged and modeled? Is it more acceptable than "living in the fast lane"? Is going to church and being in Bible study the rule rather than the exception? Does peer pressure encourage deviate behavior or bring out the best of the spiritual dimension of the soldier? Are we helping turn America back to a Nation "Under God" by encouraging our soldiers to find spiritual roots? All these questions reflect on the spiritual climate.

Religious support is a charge given to the Unit Ministry Team (UMT), the chaplain and his or her enlisted assistant, by doctrine. Many commanders fail to realize that there is a difference between command responsibility and support. Consequently, many commanders and leaders abdicate their rightful role in the spiritual development of their units. The UMTs assist the commander—it is the commander's responsibility. This is one responsibility that cannot be delegated because the commander and senior NCOs determine the spiritual climate. The mere act of delegating one's spiritual responsibility reveals the level of importance placed on spiritual development.

The mission of the UMT was described in the Army Trainer by a maneuver analyst for the Army's Combined Arms Training Activity, Fort Leavenworth, Kansas as follows:

> The UMT's mission on the Airland battlefield is to provide comprehensive religious, moral, and spiritual support to soldiers and their units. The UMT assists the commander by facilitating spiritual factors that enable soldiers to strengthen their faith. Thereby they achieve inner stability and peace. Inner strength reinforces the bond among soldiers and enhances both individual and group spiritual awareness. A proactive UMT fosters unit cohesion; this ultimately encourages high motivation, thorough dedication, and effective performance among its members.[72]

Army doctrine states that: Chaplains and chaplain assistants are normally assigned on a one-to-one basis. In smaller units chaplain section is comprised of one chaplain and one chaplain assistant who together constitute the "Unit Ministry Team [UMT]."[73] Units with healthy spiritual climates within their command climate would say the Unit Ministry Team consists of the commander, the chaplain, and the chaplain's assistant. The commander alone is the single most important factor in establishing the spiritual climate.

Strong spiritual climates within organizations are characterized as having commander involvement, providing freedom of ministry action for the UMT, allocating time and training resources, and being open to spiritual organizations that assist in the spiritual development of the soldier.

The UMT is a tremendous resource but not an end in itself. Combat can shake the underpinnings of life, and the UMT is essential to the unit's ability to handle crisis situations. Chaplains must share the soldiers' world and be in constant contact. Many soldiers have no religious foundation and their backgrounds have immunized them against hope. Pastoral care and counseling are invaluable under these conditions. Others seek meaning and faith. Many question religious beliefs and wonder why God let them down. The UMT must be free to minister.

We cannot merely talk of "command support" if we are to have the proper spiritual climate and effective unit ministry. We need to talk of "command involvement."

Our hope for the future is that the Nation's and the Army's leadership will accept their spiritual responsibilities and put a premium on spiritual readiness. Those who have a strong personal faith, lead by example based on Biblical principles, and have set the proper spiritual climate will be the ones who turn us back toward being "One Nation Under God."

CONCLUSION

This is a time for spiritual renewal in America. There is hope. We can emerge stronger than before if we will rediscover the foundational truths behind the success of our nation and our Army.

In his farewell address at West Point in 1962, General of the Army Douglas MacArthur spoke eloquently of "the crash of guns, the rattle of musketry, the strange, mournful mutter of the battlefield." He also spoke of the faith that sustains soldiers in combat: "The soldier, above all other men, is required to practice the greatest art of religious training—sacrifice. In battle and in the face of danger and death, he discloses those divine attributes, which his Maker gave when he created man in His own image. No physical courage and no brute instinct can take the place of the Divine help which alone can sustain him."[74]

Faith is critical. We must stem the spiritual decay in America. It will take leadership that acknowledges and obeys God's plan.

We need to once again become a "Nation Under God" led by men and women of faith who exhibit spiritual leadership and set a proper spiritual climate. Then and only then will we begin to turn away from relativism and secular humanism and turn back to God.

Leaders are responsible. We cannot turn over our responsibilities of spiritual leadership to the church or our chaplains. The strength of our nation and the effectiveness of our fighting forces depend on leaders that are spiritually responsible.

Great leaders are like eagles. They don't flock—one finds them one at a time. Leaders like our founding fathers are the rarest of eagles. America's founding fathers understood very well the principle that faith and freedom go together, and that one cannot survive long without the other. Their faith and strength of commitment are well documented. It is for each of us to decide the commitment we are willing to make. It will be for future generations to decide how well the commitment has been honored.

The question for each of us is: *In my lifetime, did I make a difference in the spiritual renewal of America?* Our very existence depends on it.

The mighty eagle…when his mighty wing feathers become heavy with oil and dirt and his beak and talons become calcified and brittle he retires for a period of renewal…He pulls out his feathers, extracts each claw and smashes his beak against rocks until it is gone.…When his beak, talons and feathers have regrown, he emerges in a renewed condition—stronger than before.[75]

Be an eagle.

ENDNOTES

CHAPTER 1

1. http://www.eyewitnesstohistory.com/atomictest.htm, "The First Atomic Bomb Blast, 1945"

CHAPTER 3

1. "Is America a Christian Nation?" Sermon by David Barton 2009
2. Website: www.beliefnet.com/Faiths/Faith-Tools/Meditation/2005/01/Prayers-Of-The-Presidents.aspx

CHAPTER 6

1. *Holman Quick Source Guide to Christian Apologetics*, Doug Powell, p252–255.

CHAPTER 21

1. "What Does God know?" W. L. Craig, p 45

CHAPTER 22

1. en.wikipedia.org/wiki/Arthur Andersen
2. Ibid.

CHAPTER 25

1. *Israel My Glory* magazine: Jan/Feb 2010 "The Kingdom of the Beast" pp 22 Charles E. McCracken
2. *Israel My Glory* magazine: Jan/Feb 2010 "The Emergent Kingdom" pp 27–28 Gary Gilley
3. Ibid. Gilley p 27

CHAPTER 35

1. Much insight for this article came from Hal Lindsey's much-recommended, comprehensive review of the Gospel of John.

CHAPTER 37

1. Holman Quick Source Guide to Christian Apologetics, Doug Powell, p 39–41.

CHAPTER 41

1. http://scienceblogs.com/builtonfacts/2009/08/maxwells_equations_light.php

CHAPTER 44

1. Nancy L. DeMoss, *The Rebirth of America* (Arthur S. DeMoss Foundation, 1986), 75.
2. Ibid.
3. Russell F. Weigley. *New Dimensions in Military History* (California: Presidio Press, 1975), 38–72.
4. Parker C. Thompson, *The United States Army Chaplaincy—From Its European Antecedents to 1791* (Washington, 1978), 106.
5. Ibid., 175.
6. Gary T. Amos, *Defending the Declaration* (Tennessee: Wolgemuth and Hyatt Publishers, 1989), 32.

7. Verna Hall, *The Christian History of the Constitution of the United States of America* (New York: Human Science Press, 1976), 27.
8. Hart, 283.
9. Maurice W. Cranston, *John Locke: A Biography* (London: Oxford Press, 1957).
10. Ibid., 75.
11. Benjamin Hart. *Faith & Freedom* (Texas: Lewis and Stanley Publishers, 1988), 14.
12. Ibid., 78.
13. Ibid., 79.
14. Richard Tuck, N*atural Rights Theories: Their Origin and Development* (Cambridge: Cambridge University Press, 1979), 1–2.
15. Ibid.
16. Ibid.
17. Amos, 169.
18. Ibid.
19. Ibid., 170.
20. Hart., 15.
21. Alexis De Tocqueville. *Democracy in America* (New York: 1966).
22. Hart., 16.
23. Hart., 16.
24. Ibid.
25. Ibid., 18.
26. Ibid.
27. Ibid., 19.
28. Ibid.
29. Ibid., 20.
30. Ibid., 21.
31. Ibid., 22.
32. Peter Marshall and David Manuel, *The Light and the Glory* (Old Tappan, NJ: Fleming H. Revell Company), 13.

33. Ibid.
34. Ibid.
35. Hart., 24.
36. Ibid., 14.
37. Tocqueville., 155.
38. Ibid.
39. From "Be Alert to Spiritual Danger." (Chicago: Institute of Basic Youth Conflicts, 1979). 17.
40. Ibid.
41. John Price, *America at the Crossroads* (New York: Tyndale House, 1979), 12.
42. Cited in Daniel B. Jorgensen, *The Service of Chaplains to Army Air Units 1917–1946*. 277.
43. Samuel A. Stouffer, et al., *The American Soldier: Combat and its Aftermath: Studies in Social Psychology in World War II.* Vol II, 172.
44. Ibid., 173.
45. Ibid., 186.
46. John Keegan and Richard Holmes, *Soldiers: A History of Men in Battle* (New York: Viking Press, 1986), 52.
47. Hart, 273.
48. Ibid, 274.
49. *William J. Johnson, George Washington. the Christian* (Nashville, Tennessee: 1919), 55.
50. General John W. Vessey, Jr., Chairman, Joint Chiefs of Staff, from an address for the Anniversary of the Chaplain Branch given at the U.S. Army Chaplain Center and School, Fort Monmouth, NJ, 29 July 1985.
51. Jurg Martin Gabriel, *Clausewitz Revisited: a Study of His Writings and of the Debate Over Their Relevance to Deterrence Theory.* 48.
52. Keegan and Holmes, 48.
53. Ibid.

54. Ibid.
55. John Schumacher. Address given at the Baccalaureate service at the Sergeants Major Academy, 1 July 1991. "The Spiritual Dimension of Leadership."
56. Peter Paret, *Clausewitz and the State* (New York: Oxford Press, 1976), 85.
57. Ibid.
58. FM 22-100., 24.
59. James Mac Gregor Burns. *Leadership* (New York: Harper and Row, 1987), 4.
60. Schumacher.
61. Ibid.
62. Omar M. Bradley.
63. Schumacher.
64. Ibid.
65. J. Oswald Sanders. *Spiritual Leadership* (Chicago: Moody Press, 1986). 101.
66. Ibid., 37.
67. Ibid., 35.
68. Ibid., 38.
69. Ibid., 73.
70. Ibid., 82.
71. Ibid., 79.
72. Timothy R. Dicker, Cpt, *On the Battlefield: Stress, Fatigue,Fear, Army Trainer.* 13.
73. U.S. Army Combat Developments Command, *The Chaplain's Role as Related to Soldier Motivation*, 2–3.
74. Douglas MacArthur, Address to the members of the Association of Graduates, United States Military Academy at West Point, New York, 12 May 1962.
75. Cited from Betty Spooner, 1982. The "Eagle."

Acknowledgements

A special thanks to all the "Blue Collar" contributing authors:

Lela Battistini lives in Sharpsburg, Georgia and is the proud mother of five children. She owns and operates "Free at Last" Cleaning Services and provided significant editing work in the writing of this book.

Marcia Daniels is a retired Air Force major, inspirational speaker, writer, and reseller/distributor for Reliv products. She lives in Oklahoma City, OK and is a member of Bethlehem Star Baptist church where she serves as Director of Little Star school, nursery, and puppet programs.

Doug Hanson is a retired executive from The DuPont Company. Originally, from Texas where he met and married Lynne, his wife of 47 years, they have three children and nine grandchildren. He leads and participates in mission work and serves as a deacon at First Baptist church in Gainesville.

Emmett Holley lives in Gainesville, GA with his wife Ellen and his son and daughter. He owns and operates Tru-Vision enterprises, a home and commercial building and remodeling company. He is a deacon at First Baptist church in Gainesville.

Jeff McAdams was saved by the grace of God at the age of 30. His professional career has been in retail management since graduating from Appalachian State University in 1983. He is unmarried and lives in Raleigh, NC where he attends a small local assembly of believers.

Kathryn Rogers is a mother and a wife. Desiring to make a difference in another's life, she was led by the Lord to become a Stephen Minister Leader. She and her husband live in St Louis, MO and are members of Kirkwood Baptist church.

Rick Saltzer is employed as a healthcare representative in central Pennsylvania where he lives with his wife and two sons.

Zoraya Valdez lives in Gainesville, GA with her son, Eliseo. She owns and operates a lawn care and landscaping company. She recently served as interim minister for a start-up Hispanic ministry in Roswell, GA. She was ordained as a minister (transitioned from "blue collar" to "white collar") this year.

Jack Wehmiller and his wife C.J. live in Murrayville, GA. They have two sons and five grandchildren. They have served in various positions while members of First Baptist church in Gainesville for 23 years. Retired from the sales and marketing industry, Jack and C.J. are commissioned "field personnel" with the Cooperative Baptist Fellowship and Jack also works with Rivers of the World ministry.

and the permission to include significant excerpts from the study project paper "The Greatest Threat…Spiritual Decay" by then Lieutenant Colonel and now Lieutenant General **Robert Van Antwerp**

There are far too many people to list in thanks for their contribution of inspiration and support. In our Christian walk, we are all out there casting seeds, adding water, pulling weeds, tilling the ground, and assisting with the harvest. The individuals that we meet in our journey through life all contribute to our final mosaic piece of art that defines who we are. The greatest contributor and True Source, of course, is Christ.

Aside from family members and friends, there are however, several who have provided significant spiritual insight and inspiration that assisted in the creation of this book. Some are people that we've never personally met. This testifies to their illumination in the world that reaches thousands, even millions of people. May they continue to "be a bright light" and radiate mightily for the Lord.

Pastor Bill Coates	Pastor Jentzen Franklin	Dr. Jack Van Impe
Hal Lindsey	Bishop Mike McDaniel (promoted)	Pastor Andy Stanley
Pastor Charles Stanley	Pastor John Weber	

We welcome your comments. If you have any comments or a story or testimony that you want to share, then please email us at: BCF@BABRIGHTLIGHT.COM.

Bible Translation Abbreviations

New International Version	(NIV)
New Living Translation	(NLT)
English Standard Version	(ESV)
New American Standard Bible	(NASB)
International Standard Version	(ISV)
GOD'S WORD Translation	(GWT)
King James Bible	(KJB)
American King James Bible	(AKJB)
American Standard Version	(ASV)
Bible in Basic English	(BBE)
Darby Bible Translation	(DBT)
English Revised Version	(ERV)
Webster's Bible Translation	(WBT)
Weymouth New Testament	(WNT)
Young's Literal Translation	(YLT)
The Message	(MSG)

NOTE: The vast majority of all Scripture verses used in this book were referenced from the website: www.biblos.com. Any denotation of a scripture verse that does not have a specific translation is for the reader's reference only. It is a partial verse or has combined verbiage from more than one translation.